T0305325

The Development of International Business

NEW HORIZONS IN INTERNATIONAL BUSINESS

Series Editor: Peter J. Buckley, *Centre for International Business, University of Leeds (CIBUL), UK*

The New Horizons in International Business series has established itself as the world's leading forum for the presentation of new ideas in international business research. It offers pre-eminent contributions in the areas of multinational enterprise – including foreign direct investment, business strategy and corporate alliances, global competitive strategies, and entrepreneurship. In short, this series constitutes essential reading for academics, business strategists and policy makers alike.

Titles in the series include:

The Development of International Business

A Narrative of Theory and Practice

Robert Pearce

Professor of International Business Emeritus, John H Dunning Centre for International Business, Henley Business School and Department of Economics, University of Reading, UK

NEW HORIZONS IN INTERNATIONAL BUSINESS

Cheltenham, UK • Northampton, MA, USA

Published by
Edward Elgar Publishing Limited
The Lypiatts
15 Lansdown Road
Cheltenham
Glos GL50 2JA
UK

Edward Elgar Publishing, Inc.
William Pratt House
9 Dewey Court
Northampton
Massachusetts 01060
USA

A catalogue record for this book
is available from the British Library

Library of Congress Control Number: 2017939809

This book is available electronically in the **Elgar**online
Business subject collection
DOI 10.4337/9781786439987

ISBN 978 1 78643 997 0 (cased)
ISBN 978 1 78643 998 7 (eBook)

Typeset by Servis Filmsetting Ltd, Stockport, Cheshire

To My Brother Tony

Contents

Introduction and acknowledgements

The aim of the book is to provide a broad-brush overview of frameworks and methodologies that can help us to understand and evaluate the role and status of the Multinational Enterprise (MNE) in the current global economy. The fact that the context of the 'current' global economy is coming under stresses and uncertainties that have emerged since the writing began in the spring of 2016 may, indeed, add an extra dimension of relevance to the approach adopted, since key emphasis will be placed on the MNE's strong historic propensity for reactive dynamism and its possession of a strategic diversity that provides it with a range of evolutionary (rather than potentially disruptive) future options.

To address this overarching agenda the book adopts two, closely interlinked, organising themes. The first is to position our current understanding of International Business (IB) as the outcome of processes of change that we trace through roughly the past half-century. We will find the roots of our contemporary analysis and concerns emerging during the 1960s. This will conveniently underwrite the core proposition of the essential reactive adaptability of the MNE, since we can then stylise the institutional and policy contexts that conditioned the firms of that time as massively and categorically different from those faced today. Of course, in most areas of analysis and interpretation, an effective comprehension of any contemporary reality can be greatly enhanced through an understanding of from where that reality had emerged. But, quite suddenly, such knowledge of the evolutionary dynamics of IB may be taking on an enhanced and direct relevance. To a considerable degree the external contexts in which MNEs have functioned had seemed relatively settled (institutionally and ideologically) for several decades. As already suggested this no longer seems as reliably true. Knowledge of the MNE's responsive dynamic capacities and its available scopes and options seem likely to come back into play. Whereas it seems implausible to anticipate 'mirror image' regression of MNEs into one of their antecedent formats, it does seem logical to expect its future dynamics to involve some reformulation or remix of its past experience and operative formulations. If its current structures and motivations do become a step on the road to a revised status in a new global economic order how it got here will provide essential pointers.

The second main organising principle of the narrative is then to trace out the development of two seemingly mostly independent strands of analysis, designated here as 'theory' and 'practice', and then to suggest and advocate the frequent intuitive and mutually supportive interdependencies between their processes of interpretive enhancement. Given the author's career-long involvement with the 'Reading School' of IB the theoretical strand is, inevitably and unashamedly, positioned around the elements of Dunning's 'eclectic' framework. But the narrative will reflect and build on the value of this eclecticism, by tracing the ways in which separate contributions (reflecting independent roots in different areas of economics) have fed into the overall paradigm. Different aspects of the argument can then be developed to provide separate analytical insights into 'how' firms are able to become MNEs, 'when' and 'where' this led them to initiate and locate overseas value-adding activities, as well as important decisions regarding ownership and control structures.

This eclectic agenda not only points to the practical versatility of Dunning's paradigm but also to a key interpretive theme of this book. The defining purpose of IB, as it became formulated as an independent discipline, was to apply theoretically rigorous analytical constructs to the resolution of practical issues provoked by the expansion of national firms into international operations. The discipline emerged to provide orderly frameworks to elucidate a diverse and ever-changing reality.

The second, 'practical', strand then usefully reverses the analytical causation by arguing that once the broad tenets of these theory-based frameworks were in place they served very effectively to allow us to understand the origins, nature and implications of major organisational restructurings in MNEs. We can then see the MNE as a network of diverse subsidiary operations that is always open to reconfiguration as institutional and economic conditions change. We will systematise this process of evolution over the past half-century as one from a 'multi-domestic hierarchy' organisational structure (reflecting a protection dominated global economy) to a 'network hierarchy' (adapting to the potentials of freer trade and global supply networks) to the 'heterarchy or transnational' (internationalising their innovation and R&D in more heterogeneous and strategically diverse structures). Whereas the established theoretical modalities provided for a prompt and informed analysis of such evolving structures, the process of understanding such new dimensions of organisation and strategic complexity also fed back to an enrichment of the theoretical perspectives themselves; theory and practice in IB evolved together. The book can then conclude by reverting to a major objective by showing how the analytical intermeshing of the theoretical and practical strands – as well as acceptance of their mutually contingent interactions with the MNE's external environment – can help us to formalise ways of evaluating the performance implications of these firms for explicit and implicit stakeholders. This too may take on new or revised facets as the national and international contexts face unexpected changes and forces.

As always, my greatest debt in production of the manuscript is to Jill Turner who typed it with her usual accuracy and patience. I am also grateful to Nick Turner for 'sorting out' the figures!

Robert Pearce
Reading
January 2017

1. Multinationals: in theory and practice

INTRODUCTION

The academic discipline and research agenda that we now designate as International Business (IB) emerged in a gradual, almost subliminal, way during the 1960s. We can here accept the widely held view that the decisive starting point for this theoretical process was the completion of Stephen Hymer's PhD thesis in 1960 and then locate the most clear-cut evidence of its provisional maturity in two conferences held at the end of the decade that, for the first time, took firms with international operating perspectives as their central theme. In terms of theorising Hymer's defining transformative insight was the need to replace a visibly redundant macro-level theory of foreign direct investment (FDI) with a micro-level theory of (what we came to call) the Multinational Enterprise (MNE), initially perceived as the firms that did FDI. But, for the purposes of the narrative we will develop here, the way Hymer did this is crucially indicative. By confronting observed *practicalities* of the world he could study in the 1950s he both demonstrated the manifest inadequacies of the dominant existing *theory* and also showed how elements of the newly observed reality not only negated the earlier perspective, but also provided precise insights towards the genesis of revised theorising.[1]

During the 1960s interest in IB progressed, at least initially, through an often ad hoc series of intuitive and informal interactions between a growing group of scholars bringing a range of differently focused, mainly practically based, insights into a discussion of the behaviour of these internationalised firms. The two conferences referred to earlier became a testament to the fact that, by the end of the decade, there were enough recognised scholars with acknowledged expertise in the area to allow for the assembly and exchange of high-quality knowledge and facilitate rewarding debate. The titles of the conferences and their published volumes also testified that, beyond doubt, the agenda was now firmly focused on the firms, with Charles Kindleberger (1970) referring to the International Corporation[2] and John Dunning (1971) to the Multinational Enterprise.[3] But whereas the central aims of the conferences and the overarching interests of their convenors/editors was to build a coherent understanding of these firms (working towards a theory) the range of contributors, and their intellectual origins, also underlined that to do this realistically needed to draw in multifaceted aspects of their practice and the contexts in which they were learning to operate.

It is also very indicative of the ad hoc formulation of early insights into what we now consider to be IB that what became its single most influential contribution from the 1960s, Raymond Vernon's Product Cycle Model (1966), was in no way, shape or form intended as such, and originated from very different concerns. In terms that we *would* now recognise, Vernon's concern was, in effect, to investigate the macro-level relationship between FDI and trade. What emerges though is that in order to understand the bases of the relationship it is necessary to understand the capacities and the motivations of the firms that do the FDI. Indeed, in a way that precisely presages a central concern of our narrative here, Vernon shows that whether FDI complements or substitutes for trade depends on the practicalities of the specific motivation pursued by the MNE's operation; whether it is efficiency seeking (complementarity) or market seeking (substitution). Feeding back into theory we will see how this aspect of strategic practice affects the performance implications (on firms and locations) of IB.

This 'early days' preamble, in fact, already points towards the two key themes that will underpin and motivate our narrative of the ways in which IB, in theory and practice, went on to evolve into the analytical and operative reality we need to understand and address today. The first of these themes is that in order to comprehend and evaluate the operation of the international economy it is necessary to accept the MNE as the emblematic agent in determining its functioning and outcomes. Whereas national and international institutions and policies are clearly central in conditioning the potentials of the international economy, it is the MNE whose innate nature is most oriented to building these opportunities into its own strategic imperatives and competitive behaviour. Theory has always told us that national economies differ in terms of their formulation and sources of competitiveness and that the international economy works best where these distinctive national comparative advantages can be most effectively realised globally. What mainstream theorising seemed reluctant to recognise was just how often these *national* potentials were activated by MNEs towards their *internationalised* competitive imperatives. The emergence of IB as a (perhaps unnecessarily) independent area of theorising set out to address this lacuna in mainstream economics by building frameworks and analytical structures that could distinguish the nature of the MNE as a distinctive agent actively operating very much within the wider perceptions of the global economy. Many of the major contributors to the theoretical approaches we will review here were, unreservedly, economists addressing issues they defined as economics; this certainly applies to those (Hymer, Dunning, Vernon, Kindleberger) we have already cited. Overall, we argue, the ultimate objective of the IB strand we aim to develop here is, therefore, to achieve an understanding of the MNE as an agent in the global economy; its objectives there, how it is able to go about their achievement, and the implications of this for the global economy and its constituent national economies.

The second key theme is that for IB to serve these analytical purposes it needed to be based around an understanding of the MNE that precisely encompassed its reality; what it really looked like, how it really behaved as a competitive entity, what attributes allowed it to do so. There was no real room in IB theorising to see its main player, the MNE, as in any way a convenient abstraction (as much of its analysis had tended to cast FDI). The starting point needed to be the MNE as a practical form, with comprehension of this then focusing on *how* it could undertake the step of internationalising its operations, *when* it decided to do so, *where* it chose to operate and *what* it expected to achieve through its own abilities and decisions. These concerns were not, of course, inherently anathema to mainstream economics and, as we will see, aspects of its thinking and methodologies feed positively into the propagation of IB's own analysis. Nevertheless, the formulation of IB as a discipline operating at a certain degree of analytical distance from mainstream analysis did depend on its willingness to start from and accept the precise *practical* nature of its main player (the MNE) as a perhaps inconsistent, messy and always evolving real-world presence.

Though the theorising we will adopt here operates at a selectively informed distance from the established methodologies and models of mainstream international economics we will see that ultimately our objective is an essentially economic one; to understand and evaluate the relationship between MNEs and national economies (or, sometimes, specifically defined locations in them) and how this is mediated by the wider institutional context of the global economy. But the particular strength we will advocate for IB theorising is then its focal emphasis on building its analysis from an informed understanding of the reality of MNEs as the operative players, and the evolving contexts from which they have emerged and learnt to function in; we eschew abstractions and assumptions not informed by observed reality.

Responding to these perspectives an important theme within our narrative of the development of IB has been the beneficial interleaving of its practice and its theory. The enriching of vital elements of the relevant theoretical frameworks' generation has come about from the perceived necessity of explaining and encompassing new facets of the way MNEs were actually behaving in practice. But, at the same time, understanding and evaluating how and why the operating reality of MNEs was actually changing immediately benefitted from application of the formulations of the theory itself. The main *theoretical* basis of our exposition of the competitive nature of the MNE will be Dunning's (1977, 1988, 1993; Dunning and Lundan, 2008) eclectic framework. This allows us to focus initially on the sources of the firms' ability to expand internationally; that is, their ownership advantages (OAs). Then we move to those factors that lead to the decision to implement this step and to the choice of locations for these geographically extended operations. These are location advantages (LAs). The third element of the framework then addresses a key characteristic in their expanding organisation. Their ability to benefit competitively from the internalisation of the markets for intermediate goods, including OAs. This is described as an internalisation advantage (IAs). Then the aspect of MNE *practice* that we trace through time is how they have organised for global competitiveness through networks of subsidiaries. These, we emphasise, can address very different strategic motivations that will evolve within the overall competitive restructuring of MNEs as their internal competences develop and as the global environment they target changes.

This chapter ends by providing a definition of IB's principal subject; the MNE. Chapter 2 begins our narrative of its evolution and elucidation with the presentation of two, closely interrelated, pioneering arguments deriving from the insights of Hymer. Firstly, we demonstrate how Hymer projected the need for a theory of the MNE from a careful analysis of the inability of antecedent theories of FDI to explain realities observable in the 1950s. Secondly, from Hymer's advocation of the need to place specific sources of firm-level competitive advantage at the centre of MNE theorising we derive Dunning's ownership advantage (OA) as the first element in his OLI framework. Two further perspectives are then derived from this. Firstly, a characterisation of OAs that indicates that these are most likely to be intangible competitive attributes that are expensive to create, but then very inexpensive to use (notably as a source of the ability to venture into international operations). Secondly, that this interpretation of OAs can be effectively modelled in Hymer's argument that MNEs are very likely to occur in highly concentrated industries, with clear pointers to the presence of oligopolistic forces in their competitive behaviour.

Whilst these Hymer-based pointers were being moulded into the first phase of a more widely positioned framework in IB, Vernon's (1966) product life-cycle model (the subject of Chapter 3) had emerged as an, initially, standalone contribution that, we can now see, provided insights that would mesh very valuably with both the theoretical and practical faces of our investigation. Indeed, we can see both those dimensions as clearly and distinctly central to Vernon's approach. The initial impetus to the analysis was to address a perceived *theoretical* issue in international economics; the relation between FDI and trade. But at the core of his approach to doing so was an accepted *practical* perception; the life cycle of a product from its market-dominating inception (innovation) to its status as a mass-market standardised good sold in a very price-sensitive market. Here the way Vernon modelled the innovation process proved to be valuable in two ways. Firstly, it provided an informed view of how OAs could be formulated in what would become an MNE's home country. At the same time it set out a template for the organisation of innovation that (as we will see in Chapter 7) could transfer into the way these firms would eventually approach product development as an internationalised function.

Then, as we will elaborate in Chapter 3, Vernon's explanations for the types of international activity adopted in the 'mature' and 'standardised' product stages of the PLCM provide us with very neat pointers towards the more wide-ranging perspectives of MNE's organisational structures and their revisions that we will address in Chapter 4. Once successful innovation had given firms products of sufficient competitive maturity to generate significant demand in other, relatively high-income, markets Vernon expects this to lead to production in those markets. The main determinant for this relocation of supply would be the costs of trade (protection and transport) so that, in our terms, the motivation would be market seeking (MS). But if, by Vernon's writing in the mid-1960s (mainly) US MNEs had adopted this approach to the supply of several foreign markets we have what Chapter 4 will discuss as the multi-domestic hierarchy (MH) MNE organisational form. Isolated local-market-focused subsidiaries each compete exclusively for the domestic market of their own host economy.

But these scenarios were very much blighted by the inefficiencies endemic to a highly protectionist international economy with production artificially fragmented between many separate locations. The narratives of Chapters 3 and 4 encompass different responses to this through the emergence of the efficiency-seeking (ES) motivation pursuing new dimensions of competitiveness. Within the compass of Vernon's model this imperative towards ES supply is reached when the focal product has moved through its life cycle to the 'standardised good' stage. Here it has now become a mass-market good with many rival suppliers, so that cost-efficient price-competitive manufacturing becomes the major objective. This now requires a separation between where the good is produced (low-cost location) and where it will be sold (more prosperous market). For this to be viable Vernon adopted the expectation of a freer-trade situation facilitating such intra-group trade.

The actual emergence of such a development, we can now see, also provided the impetus for the decline of MS strategy (and of the multi-domestic hierarchy) and its replacement by the ES imperative (in what becomes a network hierarchy). As our discussion in Chapter 4 will elaborate the moves towards a freer-trade environment drove this process from two sides. Firstly, it removed the protection that inefficient MS subsidiaries had received and, thereby, rendered this positioning increasingly vulnerable as a dominant organising strategy for MNEs. But, at the same time, it facilitated the emergence of a new subsidiary-level positioning that could use the newly available trade options. Thus the subsidiaries could undergo a metamorphosis to the export-oriented ES role, where efficient production (based around a host-country's major sources of comparative advantage) feeds into their group's integrated global supply network. They become integral to MNEs' reconfiguration as network hierarchies (NH).

In theoretical terms we can see the differing postures of MS and ES subsidiaries as responsive to two different categories of LAs; negative LAs for MS and positive LAs for ES. This is elaborated, and its implications developed, in Chapter 5 through the analysis of Kojima (1978). In its analytical essence Kojima's models reverted to the more macro-level concern of the relationship between FDI and trade though, as we will emphasise in Chapter 5, this can be rewardingly interpreted in IB terms so that, we will assert, it becomes a valuable and clarifying contribution to our comprehension and evaluation of MNE behaviour in different contexts. This feeds, particularly strongly, into how our view of different conditioning LAs delineates the circumstances determining MNEs' approach to their globalised operations. Thus we will project Kojima's 'trade-destroying FDI' as describing our world of the MH, where a predominantly protectionist international economy (negative LAs) fragmented MNE production into a multiplicity of, innately inefficient, isolated and localised subsidiaries. Then, in contrast, the opening of the global economy and of its constituent locations provides the context for 'trade-creating FDI' where efficiency-targeting subsidiaries (activating host-country comparative advantages or positive LAs) enter into international supply networks.

In Chapter 6 we complete our presentation of the basic elements of Dunning's eclectic framework with a discussion of aspects of internalisation theory, building on the defining insights of Buckley and Casson (1976). This projects the positioning of 'internalisation' in theorising the MNE as reflecting imperfections in the markets for many intermediate goods so that these firms often organise such transactions within the firm, rather than operating as either a seller or buyer in a market transaction for such an intermediate. This points towards a distinction we offer, in

Chapter 6, between 'outward' and 'inward' internalisation. In these terms Dunning's initial adoption of internalisation saw OAs as vital intermediate goods, whose use in an overseas FDI operation would render the firm an MNE. But, as was well known by the early 1970s, international markets for such OAs (licensing of technology, management contracts, trademark licensing, franchising) did exist. Internalisation theory needed to explain how firms that chose to become MNEs decided to forego the market option and, instead, to internalise the 'outward' transfer of such OAs. Here Buckley and Casson (1976) elaborate the case of technology as a potentially marketable OA that, in practice, was frequently internalised in ways that impelled the extension of the firm as an MNE.

What we then call 'inward' internalisation occurs where a firm decides to build the supply of inputs (components, raw materials, energy, services) into its controlled scope, rather than purchase them in an open market transaction. Chapter 6 invites us to revisit the role of OAs in another way, adding to its original definition in Chapter 2. Thus we will argue that a key attribute of OAs (in essence what Dunning designated as a 'transaction' OA) is the ability to organise and benefit from acts of internalisation. Many 'inward' internalisation opportunities (for example, access to raw materials or component parts supply) are initially available to several competitors in an industry. Possession of a superior ability to detect and act on such an opportunity can be considered as an OA, independent of the internalisation benefits that come on tap once the transaction is completed.

If Chapter 6 completes the basic introduction of our main *theoretical* framework (Dunning's OLI) then Chapter 7 does the same for our dominant framework for strategic *practice,* by adding knowledge seeking (KS) to our earlier emphasis on MS and ES. Central to this is that, for both firms and economies, the sustainability of their development and competitive upgrading needs the generation of, or access to, new sources of knowledge. In the latter decades of the twentieth century more and more countries came to address these needs through the generation of 'national systems of innovation' (NSI). These established the institutions of new knowledge creation (for example, research laboratories in firms or universities) and the mechanisms for moving such knowledge towards active development of path-breaking new goods and services. This led to technological and market heterogeneity on a global basis, since the most successful NSI were those that generated genuinely unique and distinctive sources of new innovation-oriented knowledge.

But this meant that for MNEs, aiming to access new sources of creative potentials towards their own competitive enrichment, it became necessary to investigate such possibilities in a range of different locations with the aim of drawing selections of these into their own innovation agendas. This engendered the emergence of KS as an increasingly internationalised component of their competitive strategies. Chapter 7 discusses, in some detail, how MNEs have addressed these new imperatives through the articulation of, sometimes interactive but often independent, globalised approaches to both R&D and innovation.

An important subtext through the narrative to be developed in this book has been the ways in which the formulations and refinement of theoretical approaches to IB have been impelled by the need to encompass, and respond to changes in, the practicalities of its operating context. A very important contemporary phenomenon which both challenges aspects of established theorising and which needs to be explained is the growth of MNEs from emerging economies. The conundrum is then that these MNEs are appearing whilst their home countries can still be described as 'emerging'. This means that in terms of expectations derived from traditional theorising these MNEs are internationalising well before the maturing of their home economy would be expected to have generated the conditions to allow them to do so. Using the case of China, Chapter 8 seeks to elucidate both the nature of these new MNEs as a challenge to traditional theory and to indicate how the enigma can be addressed by logical extensions of the mature theorising.

Central to this is to see the emergence of these new MNEs as being integral to the ongoing dynamics of their home-country's development, rather than being seen simply as an organic manifestation of a certain level of achievement in this process, as was implicit in theorising on the traditional MNEs. Thus the core of the analytical challenge of these MNEs is that they are seen to be targeting internationalisation well before the level of development of their home economy should have allowed them to generate OAs of sufficient strength and distinctiveness to enter in a truly competitive way into international operations. The offered resolution of this seeming paradox comes in two stages. Firstly, the firms are able to expand in this way because of home-country government supports (access to capital, foreign exchange, diplomatic support) that help mitigate against the competitive limitations of their in-house capacities (OAs). Then, secondly, it is necessary to explain why they are able to avail themselves of this support. This, we will argue, is because they are seen as the best means of accessing, through carefully tailored and supported acts of FDI, resources needed to help overcome emerging bottlenecks in their national development. In the China case Chapter 8 elaborates two of these strategic motivations built into the MNEs' government-assisted projects. Firstly, resource seeking, to alleviate threatened shortages in access to resources vital to the sustainability of current modes of development. Secondly, knowledge seeking, to attempt to obtain new sources of innovation-supporting competences that can help build new dimensions of national development beyond those currently prevailing.

The ever-increasing visibility of MNEs as a key agent in the evolving global economy, and the concomitant deepening of their role in mediating the ways individual national economies are positioned in that wider economy has always provided concern, both inside and outside the confines of IB theorising, over the implications of their behaviour and performance. We conclude our narrative in Chapter 9 by suggesting four distinctive generic issues that can usefully be distinguished within that wider concern. Two of these can be seen as being purely economic and with their roots in many aspects of our earlier discussion. Firstly, *efficiency* from a static optimising perspective. Do the operations of MNEs (how they apply their current OAs) improve or compromise the allocative and productive efficiency of use of the world's fixed supply of productive capacities at a point in time? Secondly, the scopes for *growth and development*, based around expansion, and improved efficiency in the use, of these resource potentials through time. Does MNEs' pursuit of their own dynamic needs and possibilities on an increasingly internationalised basis (KS) enhance or constrain these potentials?

A more political-economic issue that nevertheless builds from roots in the economic concerns is that of *distribution*. Given that MNEs' participation, along with capabilities of host locations, may generate discernible improvements in efficiency or assist in improved development performance, how are these gains distributed between the parties that contributed to them? Though our discussion in Chapter 9 will be able to set out clearly the nature of theoretical concerns over the fairness of distribution it will also suggest why their resolution in practice is so difficult. The core of this, we will argue, is the difficulty of achieving a means of evaluating the inputs from both parties. For MNEs their inputs tend to be intangible OAs that are not amenable to market pricing. For host economies MNEs' access to the relevant local resources may be distorted (in terms of price or other favourable conditions) for policy-based reasons.

Finally, at a more purely political level, there is a pervasive concern that MNEs are often able to undermine the *sovereignty* of host economies, in terms of their ability to achieve the objectives of implemented policies, or even sometimes to fully complete the generation of policies to address predetermined (maybe electorally mandated) aims. Two characteristics of MNEs can be articulated as reasons for such concern; their sheer economic strength (hegemonic OAs) and the flexibility they can proclaim or leverage as players with a range of global options. A plausible context for MNEs to exercise such powers is that of bargaining with host locations.

Here an asymmetry of information may be prevalent. MNEs can often *assert* their strengths and alternative options without having to fully reveal details of these to hosts. By contrast, hosts may need to reveal, in much more complete detail, what they can offer to MNEs. In a sense then MNEs may 'win' bargains in ways that subvert the sovereign decision scopes of locations and, indeed, may also negatively distort the implied distribution outcomes.

DEFINITION

We can define the Multinational Enterprise (MNE) as 'a firm that owns or controls value-adding activities in two or more countries'. This wording aims at a succinct precision that can nevertheless recognise the extent of the strategic scope and organisational diversity of the MNE and International Business (IB). Three elements of the definition can then be usefully elaborated to reflect this.

Firstly, the definition specifies 'value-adding activities'. This acknowledges that the ability of a firm to provide value to its ultimate consumers derives from a very large range of functional activities and that the location of *any* of these outside its home country will provide status as an MNE. Acceptance of this in pioneering definitions of the MNE may have served mainly for rhetorical completeness, since the early analysis did tend to see MNEs' dispersed operations as activated around the supposed core activities (production; direct supply of services) with all the key strategic scopes (notably innovation and the creation of competitiveness) retained in the home country. But the definition did, of course, prove admirably prescient since, as will be a central theme here, a crucial feature of the repositioning of the MNE in subsequent decades has specifically been the decentralisation of many of such strategic functions. Indeed the recent emphasis on 'global value chains' fits precisely within the definition of the MNE.

A second carefully nuanced part of the definition refers to the value-adding activities being 'owned or controlled'. Early repositioning of analytical focus from FDI to the MNE may have retained a residual myopic focus on capital, so that ownership of dispersed activities briefly remained prioritised. However, the analytical focus soon took two steps that allowed an escape from this. Firstly, it was accepted that for the firms involved the value of ownership was only that it was a means of securing control over such dispersed activities. Secondly, it was then recognised that ownership was by no means the only, or most relevant, means of activating the degree of control desired. What lay behind both these steps was the growing acceptance that what was driving the international expansion of MNEs was the need and ability to utilise firm-specific sources of competitiveness (for example, technology, skills or expertise). These competitive attributes could themselves be isolated as intermediate goods and right to their use transferred to another firm, but under contractual terms (for example, licensing agreements for technology) that placed specified constraints on how that firm could use them. A desired degree of control is retained without ownership of the activity. Once again this perception has gained widespread traction in the ideas of global supply networks or value chains. In these a dominating MNE may desire overarching control of the whole network or chain and determine its aims, but allow the participation of independent enterprises that are nevertheless constrained contractually to particular predetermined interdependent roles in the process.

The third point to elaborate here is that the definition refers to 'two or more countries'. Setting aside the small number of firms considered to have two home countries and accepting that MNEs are still routinely associated with a specific home, this thereby indicates that only one value-adding activity in one location abroad is needed to secure this status. In our practical perceptions this is an unrealistically low target to delineate firms that are likely to operate in the ways now associated with truly *multinational* enterprises. The point, however, is that there is no other threshold that would reflect a theoretical or conceptually rigorous basis. Thus beyond this low-level theoretical definition practical conceptualisations of the MNE have been research-based and pragmatic. Notably, the first extensive programme of collection of firm-level information on the MNE (Vaupel and Curhan, 1969, 1974) used six countries as an operative cut-off point. This in practice met little resistance and research derived from it had considerable acceptance and influence (Knickerbocker, 1973; Flowers, 1976; Graham, 1978). But this did not mean six was agreed as in any sense theoretically 'correct'. It did not mean that seven could be rejected as too many or five as too few.

NOTES

1. It can, in fact, be plausibly argued that the 'practical' strand of this narrative can be placed a little earlier with the publication of Dunning's (1958) detailed survey and case analysis of the operations of US firms operating in the UK.
2. The papers presented in Kindleberger (1970) derived from a symposium held at the Sloan School of Management at the Massachusetts Institute of Technology in spring 1969. In addition to three chapters addressing issues in theorising the 'International Corporation' other sections covered issues in practicalities such as 'finance and technology' and 'law and politics' and country and industry case studies.

3. The papers presented in Dunning (1971) derived from a conference held at the University
    of Reading from 28–30 May 1970. As well as papers aiming to contextualise the
    'Multinational Enterprise' appropriate practical issues addressed included 'labour rela-
    tions', 'trade and balance of payments', 'less developed countries' and 'government
    relations'.

2. From FDI to the MNE: Hymer and the roots of ownership advantage

As has proved to be logical and convenient we find the foundations of thinking on the MNE as a distinctive and influential agent in an evolving global economy in the PhD research of Hymer (1960/1976). Here we focus on two innately interlinked strands in Hymer's analysis. The first phase of this comprised a detailed critique of the antecedent macro-level models of FDI flows, discerning the ways in which this approach failed to explain observable phenomena of the post-war years. This led to his advocation of the need for a micro-level modelling of, in effect, the MNE. At a direct level, it could then be argued, any continuing interest in explaining FDI flows per se would be greatly facilitated by an understanding of the motivations and organisation of the firms that did it. But it was quickly realised, not least by Hymer himself in his later work (Hymer, 1970, 1972), that a fully informed and realistic modelling of the MNE helped address a much wider range of concerns in economics and public policy. The second phase of Hymer's work at the PhD stage was then to project from specific aspects of his critique of FDI theory some decisively influential ideas on how the 'new' theory of the MNE should proceed.

HYMER'S CRITIQUE OF THE MACRO-LEVEL THEORY OF FDI

For the purposes of this analysis and to emphasise the key points in Hymer's critique, we can adopt a quite simple and stylised version of the macro-level theory of FDI. This asserted that FDI would flow from capital-rich to capital-poor countries. This would implicitly reflect the presence of two mirror-image scenarios. Firstly, there is a group of already developed/industrialised economies. Their success is manifest in reinvestable profits generated by many extant enterprises and in personal savings by significant proportions of the population. A capital surplus is available for investment. But, the scenario then asserts, diminishing returns on capital will have set in. The most rewarding projects and opportunities are fully realised and only less certain and more marginal possibilities remain. With any deepening of domestic investment thus deemed of limited potential a *geographical* widening of search emerges. Enterprise looks for overseas opportunities.

Then the second group of countries reverse the situation. Here the key conditioning feature is not success but potential. These countries are seen to possess considerable exploitable opportunities but, because of their current very low levels of development and income, do not have the investable capital to secure their realisation. This provides the logical positioning for receipt of FDI. Overall, the characterised positioning of the two groups of countries generates an almost gravitational force, where FDI flows out of the countries that no longer provide adequate sources of renewed profitability and into those where such potentials remain latent.

Researching in the late 1950s Hymer drew on the then rather sporadic and disparate pieces of available evidence on FDI in order to assess the persisting viability of the macro-level interpretation. Methodologically it is worth noting that, whilst the data constraints precluded an overarching 'test' of the FDI theory, Hymer's more piecemeal exploration allowed for the production of a range of differently focused reservations and dissents. These, we will argue here, provided his critique with the scope to not only illustrate the severe limitations of the macro approach but to also point very clearly towards important dimensions of a new approach based around an analysis of the MNE. Hymer's work, we suggest, provides the first major illustration of how the evolution of IB theorising has persistently interfaced reactively with observed reality; our most valuable comprehensions of the MNE have been derived not as assumption-based abstractions but as responses to ways in which extant models or frameworks have been perceived to inadequately (or no longer) explain the facts.

Here we select four strands of Hymer's critique, which, whilst decisively demonstrating limitations of the 'old' theory, also very precisely define challenges that the 'new' theory would need to address and/or provide clear pointers as to how it may do so. The first of these is that the dominant directions for FDI flows in the immediate post-war years were both ways across the Atlantic; with US FDI in Europe *and* European FDI in the USA. This comprised FDI between essentially capital-rich countries and defies the prediction of the macro-theory with, indeed, relatively little FDI then flowing to the capital-poor developing economies. Projecting forward from the time of Hymer's writing we can see this phenomenon replicated in other contexts. As European recovery and integration took hold it encompassed significant growth in intra-European FDI flows, again between countries at relatively comparable income levels. It is also worth noting here that this manifested another analytical challenge that IB theorising needed to address; as the potential for trade expansion grew

FDI flows also increased. Here FDI seemed to *complement* trade rather than *substitute* for it, as some earlier analytical and historical perspectives had suggested. Eventually, Japan's FDI also provides a challenging narrative. After a first wave of FDI, which, as we will discuss later (Chapter 5), did indeed resemble the 'old' story (that is, into capital-poor economies with discernible competitive and developmental potentials), its later expansions were into North America and Western Europe. As Japan became more developed its FDI horizons seemed to expand into similar, rather than different, economies.

The FDI flow data can also be seen to have challenged a second presumption derived from the macro-level theory. If capital availability were the defining determinant of FDI then a country would either export capital (reflecting a 'surplus') or import it (because it already has the opportunities to fully utilise its domestic capital sources). No country would logically export and import FDI; gross flows would also be the net flows. Yet the data cited by Hymer clearly reflects North American and European countries both generating outward FDI and hosting inward FDI. Then, moving forward several decades, we see the alternative challenge emerging from the other side of the supposed dichotomy. In recent years very significant amounts of outward FDI have emerged from economies at relatively early stages of their development and where the needs of that process might have been assumed to have the capacity to productively absorb all domestically generated capital. Once again the message (Chapter 8) is that we need to move analytically beyond the macro-level conditions that define capital availability and instead to see FDI as one – often rather tactical or subservient – element of the behaviour of firms where internationalisation decisions reflect a wider range of needs and scopes.[1]

In a further piece of his data exploration Hymer analysed the industrial composition of inward and/or outward FDI for that quite small group of countries for which such information was then available. A clearly indicative conclusion that derived from this was that for some industries participation in FDI stocks or flows was considerable and seemingly systematic, whilst for others it was negligible with these industries mainly domestically self-contained. This, therefore, not only again undermined the perspective that FDI was uniquely driven by capital availability but also pointed towards an industry-level dimension. Certain characteristics (independent of national source) tend to generate FDI and others do not. As we will see shortly Hymer's preferred characteristic was industry concentration, with more concentrated industries likely to be more prone to generate internationalisation through flows of FDI.

The last observation we draw from Hymer's critique was, at the time, merely anecdotal or case-study-based but can now be seen to depict a crucial element of the 'real world' of FDI as implemented, we would now say, by MNEs. This demonstrated that individual acts of FDI did not, inevitably or routinely, involve international capital movements; they did not occur merely in reflection of the possibility of moving capital from an investing country into a host country. Thus, for example, European FDI in the USA was often financed, at least partly, from the New York stock exchange. This, Hymer suggested, took the analytical challenge to the *firm*-level and asked the question as to how such firms could achieve this. How could they not only convince themselves of the viability of FDI in a foreign economy but also persuade local investors of this? This, he then argued, could only occur in reflection of the possession of unique firm-level sources of competitive advantage. These could not only be leveraged to enable firms to implement their new competitive activities in an overseas location but also be projected to potential investors in a way that would enable them to raise capital wherever proved most favourable (including, at their discretion, either their home country or the new host).

We can now discern two major perceptions from Hymer's critique that decisively point the way forward into the foundations of new micro-level theorising of the MNE. Firstly, that the firms that seek to make the step into internationalisation would need distinctive firm-specific sources of competitiveness to do so and, secondly, that such enterprises are most likely to emerge in highly concentrated industries. As we will show, these two perceptions can be drawn together analytically to provide us with a starting point for the more detailed exposition of theorising on the MNE and IB. However, before that, it is useful to take a last look at the macro theory of FDI, to show how the context it sought to explain can now be better elucidated with elements of what became IB theorising. Though the FDI approach emerged in the 1930s it is clear that the dominant reality it sought to model reflected the extensive FDI growth of the half-century up to 1914; that is, during what is now designated as the 'first wave' of globalisation. Here the predominant flows of FDI were indeed between groups of countries that possessed very different characteristics that certainly provided the driving force. But we may now suggest that the dominant motivation for the FDI was that of 'resource seeking' facilitated, but not driven, by capital access factors.

In this alternative interpretation we see FDI flowing from 'northern' industrialising economies that needed to externally access important inputs into their manufacturing processes, in the form of primary resources (fuels; minerals; agricultural products). The mainly 'southern' economies that were the most plausible sources of these resources tended to be pre-industrial, in the sense of neither possessing industries capable of using their resources or, often, the ability to extract them or secure their effective cultivation. It was thus in the interest of the industrial economies to expedite the exploration of these resource potentials. But, as we now know, this needed to be activated by *firms* with the competences to secure the effective realisation of the specific potentials; experience in different types of mining and extractive expertise or in any of a range of agricultural activities. Though the needs of the investing *economy* could underwrite the desirability and plausibility of such resource-seeking investments, the *firms* still needed to be able to assert their own viability as the agents capable of implementing them. This firm-specific capacity to realise desirable potentials could then be leveraged to raise the capital to do so. Ultimately, particular *location* characteristics allow countries to attract FDI from competitively very different countries, but the effective implementation of this macro-level complementarity could only be realised by *firms* with fully realised knowledge- and skill-based competences.

Finally, we can address another aspect of the macro-theory of FDI that has been significantly negated within the IB context of recent decades. This relates to the 'old' theory's projection of outward FDI driven by a lack of new investment opportunities in the capital-rich economies. An apparently fixed stock of investment possibilities was seen as being drawn down to a residual of those with unappealing potentials. A key feature of economic performance in recent decades has been the core imperative of technological change, invoked by national policies and activated decisively by innovation-oriented enterprises (see Chapter 7). This has not, of course, negated any need for outward FDI but has instead interjected a significant new imperative for the international perspectives of globally oriented enterprises; knowledge seeking. The increasingly central role of technology and technological change in both the theory and practice of MNEs allowed for the suggestion of it as a complementary (by no means substitute) industry characteristic to sit alongside Hymer's advocation of concentration.

HYMER'S ADVOCATION: CONCENTRATED INDUSTRIES AND OWNERSHIP ADVANTAGE

We complete this section on Hymer's path-breaking contributions by introducing two very simplified models that seek to underline the ways in which his intuitive insights became projected into more formalised MNE/ IB theorising. The first of these aims to demonstrate the necessity for what became ownership advantages or firm-specific advantages by demonstrating the impossibility for MNEs to survive in perfectly competitive markets.

Central to the articulation of this is another of Hymer's seminal and persistently influential concepts; the 'liability of foreignness'.

In this first model we make three assumptions. Firstly, that the industry exists in two countries, A and B, and that in each it conforms to the conditions of perfect competition. Also the firm-level circumstances that define the industry are identical;[2] that is, in both countries the typical firm applies identical technologies through identical managerial/organisational practices and accesses identical inputs at the same prices. Secondly, that though these direct operational conditions affecting the performance of the firms are identical between the countries the social or cultural environment in which they exercise the capacities do differ in significant and influential ways. What more recent analysis would interpret as important aspects of the *institutional* context differs between countries. This can include the norms and long-established practices of the labour market, acceptable marketing and distribution practices, how to address elements of a bureaucracy as well as the legal and tax system. In any country indigenous enterprises will be well attuned to these norms but possible foreign entrants, from a background in their home-country's own institutions, norms and practices, will not be. The process of adjustment, a response to the liability of foreignness, will impose costs on a potential entrant not faced by indigenous competitors. Thirdly, something (transport costs, tariffs, other institutional restraints) precludes the possibility of trade between economies A and B.[3]

If, initially, the industry is in equilibrium in both countries so that all firms break even, there are no supernormal profits and, therefore, no incentives to new entrants. But if there is a rise in demand in, let us say, B then supernormal profits will emerge there offering, according to the assumptions of perfect competition, an incentive to new entrants. Could this, in practice, attract the expansion of firms from A into B since they have the same in-house competitive abilities and would expect to access the needed inputs on identical terms as firms from B (incumbents or new entrants)? But they should not do so since, due to the liability of foreignness, their overall cost-base is not the same as local firms. If A firms had entered they might for a while share in the industry's profitability; albeit to a lesser extent than indigenous enterprises. Then, as expanding supply draws down price in B, the A-based entrants will reach a break-even point sooner than those from B. As the latter still make some supernormal profits this will attract a few more local entrants driving price down further and the A firms into losses and exit. When the industry in B reaches its new larger equilibrium it will again be populated solely by indigenous enterprise.

Now let us change the initial assumption so that, in both countries, the industry is imperfectly competitive. Thus it is still populated by a vast number of very small firms, supplying goods or services that meet basically the same need of consumers. But the firms no longer do this in absolutely identical ways: some degree of product differentiation attracts a certain degree of consumer loyalty.[4] Within the context of still very small firms there is now some scope for different degrees of success to reflect varied competitive competences. Some firms have relative strong leadership positions,[5] others have healthy market shares that can underpin persisting survival, whilst a tail of particularly vulnerable enterprises persists at the industry's margins. Now let a rise in demand in country B again induce a generalised rise in price and the pervasive presence of supernormal profits. Once more the question emerges as to whether firms from A could become MNEs by participation in the industry's expansion in B? Now, we can suggest, the presence of competitive hierarchies in both countries can allow for this possibility. If the top-ranked firms in A, which we can now categorise as those with relatively strong ownership advantages (OAs), enter B we can suggest they may struggle to usurp much market share from the strongest B firms. These still retain a margin of competitiveness from the benefits of incumbent familiarity with the environment. But these elite A firms can, potentially, take market share from middle ranked and weaker firms in B. Their stronger OAs (internal competitive competences) *can* now outweigh the liability of foreignness to secure a sustainable status in B's market. Then, as these A firms persist in B, they can gradually embed themselves increasingly in the initially alien local conditions and bypass the liability of foreignness and build an embedded and sustainable position.

Ultimately, possession of OAs allows A-country firms to implement realistic FDI in B and become MNEs. Of course, the same logic then suggests that the reverse process is equally plausible; an expansion of the industry in A can attract stronger firms from B (with their unique OAs) to implement FDI there and also become MNEs.[6] These abstract scenarios have various important implications. Firstly, the industry becomes internationalised, with strong A-country firms increasingly an embedded part of the industry in B and vice versa. Secondly, within the limitations of this theoretical model we end up with an explanation of a challenge raised by Hymer's critique; that is, the two-way flows of FDI across the Atlantic, with A as North America and B as Europe. Thirdly, this process increased the overall influence of the firms with the strongest competitive advantages, operationalised in ways that increase the vulnerability of the weakest firms. The logic points towards increasing industry concentration as leading firms benefit from new horizons in their expansion not accessible to weaker ones. Finally, we can now provide an analytical basis for an important assertion about MNEs. These firms are only viable in less than perfectly competitive final product markets.

Our second model accepts that the most realistic operative context for MNEs is in concentrated market structures and that this provokes a role for oligopoly responsiveness within the strategic behaviour natural to these enterprises in the contemporary global economy. The starting point for this analytical scenario is a self-contained national industry, populated by a small number of very large and more-or-less equally sized firms. A long-established hegemony means that each firm is making a healthy level of profit and there is a pervasive tacit understanding to avoid destabilising the situation through aggressive competitive initiatives.

This characterisation can now be seen as intrinsically historical and, indeed, as representing an influential analytical challenge that had pre-dated, but then decisively influenced, early thinking on the MNE. The key issue – addressed in the research of Bain (1956) as adapted and developed by Hymer – was how such innately profitable concentrated industries could also remain stable in terms of an ability to avoid the challenge of new entrants. The answer to this Bain suggested lay in the fact that the incumbent firms had, over many years and at considerable expense, generated powerfully distinctive sources of competitiveness that now constituted 'barriers to entry'. The stock of such embedded and embodied knowledge and expertise was now being utilised by the mature industry participants at relatively little marginal cost.

Several staple sources of firm-level competitiveness illustrate this point. Firstly, the stock of *technologies* at the core of a firm's goods and services will have been generated in an incremental fashion over very long periods of time but can now be utilised in current supply at zero marginal cost. Furthermore, the enhancement of competitiveness is likely to be derived from evolutionary enhancement of these core sources, rather than require major new resource commitments. Secondly, a currently success-ful and competitively stable enterprise is likely to be benefitting from an experienced and balanced *management* team, operating through distinc-tive practices and procedures that have also emerged through time. This team can, and indeed will aim to, manage significant incremental growth without needing to expand itself or commit major resources to new prac-tices. Finally, such firms will be benefitting from major resources in terms of *reputation* and *marketing* expertise. This too will have been earned and learnt through time and experience and can evolve and deepen in a gradualist manner without need for radical new resource commitment or reformulation.

These in-place attributes have needed immense fixed costs in their his-torical creation but can now be applied at very low marginal cost to both current operation and incremental growth. It is the near impossibility of a new domestic competitor even attempting the inherently risky and massively expensive challenge of generating new variants of these attributes with sufficient originality to penetrate the industry that protects the incumbents and allows their profitable stability. As 'barriers to entry' this categorisation was, therefore, perceived as essentially defensive and underpinning an industry that is based around expectation of limited challenge. The emergence of theorising on the MNE, we can suggest, transforms these barriers to entry into OAs (or one of its variants) and sees them as exercised aggressively rather than as defensive preservers of an industrial status quo.

Let us now refocus our model such that the same industry also exists, in initially the same broad formulation, in another country. Here there is another group of firms that also have worked through the process of creating and successfully operationalising these forms of competitive advantage. They can observe the high profitability of the industry in our first country and feel that their own mature competitive abilities can be leveraged as new entrants there. They have already successfully undertaken the extensive costs of generating and activating the types of distinctive capacities that can be leveraged as OAs to enter the new market. Of course the marginal costs here will be far from negligible. The successful technologies may need to be adapted to adjust the goods and services to the tastes and regulations of the new host country. A local middle-level management will then need to be recruited and trained; but under the strategic initiative and guidance of the established top-level strategic team that has already secured the firm's success and articulated its ambition. Though culturally sensitive marketing and distribution procedures may also require adjustments to the firm's accepted norms it is still likely to build on proven practices and an established reputation that goes before it. It is, therefore, large and experienced firms with confidence in their expansionary potentials, which the theory now sees as their OAs, that were able to become MNEs and that the logical context for their doing so was that of concentrated industries.

We can now take this a step further, and assume a firm from the second economy does enter the first and is able to quite quickly reveal itself as representing the type of new challenge that the incumbent firms had believed their 'barriers to entry' to preclude. Now these incumbents do need to address this new and very radical challenge. One logical way of doing this is, as suggested, to also see the strengths that previously constituted their barriers to entry as now being potential OAs. They can see themselves as in a new competitive context, where a plausible direct response to the new challenger is to enter *its* home domestic market and seek to undermine its profitability there. But now other firms from *both* markets may feel challenged by this new mode of internationalised competitive aggression and feel the imperative to extend the viability of their OAs by expanding

into the 'foreign' economy. From a pair of initially complacent and competitively reserved domestic industries we now have an internationalised
two-nation oligopoly populated by a still small number of big firms (now
MNEs), that have been provoked into major new dimensions of proactive
competitiveness; the need for an international approach to strategy. At one
level we can suggest that it is the invocation of this new level of competitive
strategy that again provides us with an explanation for the two-way intra-
industry transfer of FDI that Hymer showed required an explanation.
But, of course, the operative reality of IB quickly extended beyond such
a two-economy model to the multinational, multidimensional contemporary reality of global competition. But the precepts generated here retain
their analytical value in moving us towards the capacity to understand and
evaluate this reality.[7]

THE AFTERLIFE OF OWNERSHIP ADVANTAGE

For most purposes in the development of this narrative the broad-brush
view of OAs, derived in the previous section, will suffice. Thus we see OAs
as a range of specific firm-level attributes that provide such enterprises
with the *ability* to expand internationally should they choose to do so.[8] The
OAs do not, in and of themselves, determine *when* and *where* they are operationalised in this way (this is the province of LAs) or *how* they are activated, in terms of the nature of the firm's involvement in the operations
that apply them (this is the concern of internalisation theory). However,
our willingness to simply accept OA as a wide range of firm-specific abilities with the scope to support internationalisation does run against various
long-standing attempts to refine it into discrete subcategories. Here we
will briefly comment on two of these attempts as they, to some degree,
impinge on the concerns of our wider discussion. Firstly, the distinction
between 'asset' and 'transaction' OAs and, secondly, the advocation of
'institutional' OAs.

In a neat and succinct categorisation that is very much in line with the
approach we find relevant here Eden and Li (2010) draw from the work
of Dunning 'asset-based advantages' (OA_a) which 'come from ownership or access to income-generating assets' and 'transactional advantages'
(OA_t) reflecting 'the MNE's ability to coordinate these assets with other
assets across national boundaries in ways that created competitive advantage' (2010, 29). For Dunning and Lundan (2008, 100) 'asset-specific
advantages' (OA_a) are those 'that arise from the possession of particular
intangible assets' which can be distinguished from 'transaction cost-
minimising advantages' (OA_t) 'that arise from the ability of a firm to

coordinate multiple and geographically dispersed value-added activities and to capture the gains of risk diversification'.

We can now see that the distinction between asset OAs (OA_a) and transaction OAs (OA_t) draws out two interrelated aspects of these firm-level competences which, in effect, feed back into two different aspects of our chosen definition of the MNE. Thus OA_a are distinctive knowledge-based and intangible sources of firm-specific competitiveness, which will define and underpin the precise forms that can be taken by the *value-adding* activities that are internationalised. Then OA_t will determine the ways in which the firm that owns the OA_a will participate in the overseas operation that utilises them; the extent and manner in which it *owns or controls* the value-adding activities based on its OA_a.

We can, in fact, find both *practical* and *theoretical* ways of contextualising the role of our interpretation of OA_t in understanding the MNE. In terms of evolving MNE organisational *practice* we will place central emphasis on the increasing need and ability of MNEs to leverage different value-adding activities in different locations into cohesive integrated global networks and to secure the benefits towards optimal overall performance. There would be two aspects to achieving this. Firstly, the nature of the MNE's participation in a specific part of the network; direct ownership or a degree of control exercised through a contractual arrangement. Secondly, building up and organising the intermediate goods (including OA_a) transacted between the separate nodes of the network. This does, indeed, relate to securing the benefits of common governance (economies of scale and scope) specified in Dunning's expositions though, to reiterate, we see OA_t as the *ability* to secure these benefits rather than the benefits themselves. Essentially, these are benefits that derive from the effective combinations of OA_a and LAs as mediated by OA_t.[9]

Theoretically, we can project this view of OA_t very precisely into the wider context of the OLI framework by suggesting that what it represents is the ability to secure the benefits of internalisation. The source of these benefits derives from the considerable imperfections in the markets for intermediate goods (including OA_a) and, therefore, the high levels of costs involved in trying to complete such transactions on an arm's-length or contractual basis between independent firms. Internalising the transaction between two parts of the same firm provides an alternative organisational mode that generates efficiency benefits by avoiding many of the costs of market failure. There are several elements to how the possession of effective OA_t can secure these internalisation gains, reflecting the broad perspectives of such an ability to operate within the organisational progression of MNEs as diverse competitive networks. Thus, OA_t can discern where particular intermediate goods transfers are relevant to enhancement

of the firm's networked scopes. They can evaluate where participation
in an external transaction is potentially compromised by market failures
relating to the good and secure the completion of the alternative mode
(acquisition of the potential buyer or seller). They then inculcate the
organisational practices whereby the transfer is, indeed, activated more
efficiently internal to the MNE.

In their advocation of an 'institutional' OA Dunning and Lundan
(2008) and Lundan (2010) point to the increase in MNEs' need to reach
agreements with other parties that are not themselves normally players in
markets. These can involve governments (home country or host country),
NGOs or even arrangements for non-market philanthropic activities of
the MNE. Here the MNE's objective would not normally be the most
effective arrangement for an intermediate good transfer but, instead, the
negotiation of some form of institutional arrangement that can facilitate
its ability to achieve its wider strategic objectives; though these may relate
to the conditions under which it can use its OA_a. Thus Dunning and
Lundan argued 'that the ability of the MNE to grow [now] requires effective management of both the market and non-market domains' (Lundan,
2010, 60). Indeed in Chapter 8 we will discuss a precise context – the early
emergence of MNEs from economies such as China – that involves very
close interdependence between putative MNEs and home-country institutions. But again, for the purposes of this exposition, we can suggest that
the *ability* of an MNE (established or emerging) to bargain effectively in
such institutional contexts represents another facet of its in-house managerial competences.

NOTES

1. In the preamble to their introduction of the innately micro-level construct of internalisation Buckley and Casson (1976, 11) note that 'it seems clear that recent patterns
   of investment cannot be explained by the theory that capital-abundant countries
   invest in capital-scarce countries', so that 'the post-war preference for US firms for
   investment in Europe, and the acceleration of intra-European investment and of
   European and Japanese investment in the US have to be explained by some other
   mechanism'.
2. If this were not so then a presumption that the industry is more competitive in one
   country than the other would have allowed that industry to in some way 'colonise' the
   other economy; either through trade or FDI.
3. If the industries were in equilibrium in both A and B such a cost need only be minimally
   small.
4. We can interpret the condition of an imperfectly competitive market as one where the
   value supplied to consumers is sufficiently similar between firms that no consumer could
   logically feel a need to buy the output of more than one of the firms.
5. Crucially, however, even the strongest of these enterprises remain relatively very small in
   terms of total industry size. Thus, none of this 'elite' group is big enough for any aspect

of its behaviour to be observed and interpreted as a direct challenge by other firms in the industry; we are not yet in oligopoly territory.

6. Note that in the conditions of perfect *competition* this argument does not imply oligopoly response. We do not argue that the firms in B consider entry into A *because* A firms challenged their hegemony in B. All firms are still too small to provoke such interaction. The FDI decisions taken by both groups of firms simply represent an independent response to an opportunity they objectively see opening up. They see their OAs as strong enough to facilitate sustainable entry into a foreign-market potential. As we will see this does change once industries become significantly concentrated.

7. Hymer's own subsequent (and contentious) view of this reality was to characterise the MNE as an agent innately committed to the suppression of competition and to the hegemonic control of a hierarchical segmentation of its global operations. These views are elaborated and/or contested in Dunning and Rugman (1985), Cantwell (2000), Yamin (2000), Pearce and Papanastassiou (2006).

8. We offer this emphasis on *ability* as central to our interpretation of OA in order to escape from the tendency of some presentations to define OA through the benefits their use can provide (in our view merely make possible) to MNEs, rather than in terms of the specific internal competences that can allow them to do so. An example of this is the tendency to articulate the elaboration of transaction OAs as the benefits of common governance and its contribution to the realisation of economies of scale and scope. Here we will argue that it is the *ability* to organise for the achievement of effective common governance and secure its benefits that truly represents OA$_t$.

9. Dunning and Lundan (2008) observe the amplification of securing the benefits of common governance that occurred with the emergence of increasingly decentralised structures in MNEs. The dominant source of these problems was 'the presence of innovative activity at the subsidiary level, which contributes to the overall innovativeness of the firm but also introduces agency problems and motivational conflict with the headquarters and other subsidiary units' (Lundan, 2010, 59). We will return to this in Chapter 7.

3. From innovation to internationalisation: the product cycle model

Though Hymer's PhD is now seen as the defining foundation text for a formal analysis of the MNE its core insights did not really assert that position until the early 1970s.[1] Before that, however, another, independent but valuably complementary, contribution had emerged in the form of Vernon's (1966) product life-cycle model (PLCM). In fact, as with Hymer's work, Vernon's original objective was not to develop a new mode of thinking relating to IB but rather to address an issue in the more established macro-level areas of international economics; in this case the so-called Leontief paradox relating to US trade patterns. Vernon's starting point for his investigation was that to better understand trade behaviour it is important to place this alongside an understanding of FDI and how it relates to trade. This insight, on its own, retains resonances today and the issue of whether FDI complements or substitutes for trade will pervade much of the discussion here. Nevertheless, Vernon's detailed model then, in effect, adopts the Hymeresque perception that to understand FDI and its implications it is necessary to understand the firms that do it. Though the PLCM, in and of itself, was not offered as a theory of the MNE and has not been interpreted as such, it does contain a large number of carefully projected separate insights that can be seen as underpinning future theoretical frameworks (such as OA and LA in the eclectic framework) and in the practical evolution of these firms' competitive structures (such as strategic diversity at the subsidiary level and the internationalisation of competitive strategy). It is these particular insights, as they will relate to our central themes here, that we will focus on in this exposition.

PRODUCT DEVELOPMENT (INNOVATION) STAGE

We can now see the first stage of Vernon's PLCM as providing two vital analytical insights that resonate decisively with core aspects of the theorising to come. Firstly, it provides a quite systematic and formalised indication of the processes through which the firms that will become MNEs generate the sources of competitiveness (OAs) that they will leverage in order to do so. Secondly, by placing this in a particular home country (the USA) at a particular time (the post-war years) it indicates precise elements of the nature of these advantages (the product characteristics and associated production processes). This then takes on crucial importance by indicating the types of countries that are most likely to attract their pioneering internationalisation (that is, with the most plausible location advantages).

With regard to the latter of these points two factors seem to underpin Vernon's expectations with regard to the characteristics of the firms' initial sources of competitiveness. Precisely because it becomes one of the defining achievements of the PLCM to explain how these firms undertook the crucial step from being purely national to becoming international, it is axiomatic that, at this stage, they have no reliable in-house means of detecting and accessing foreign sources of creative inputs to their own learning processes. They have no meaningful access to external market perceptions or new technologies. Innovation will be domestically motivated and sourced. Vernon then places a primary emphasis on market-driven (rather than science-driven) innovation as the source of the most successful firm-level competitive advantages, at least during the period that influenced his analysis. His underlying contextualisation here seems to have been one in which major new scientific potentials were available in significant quantities, often as spin-offs of publicly funded research originally intended for military purposes. A strong public-good element to this stock, it is implied, means that the firms most likely to innovate meaningfully from it were those whose market research could tie-up these technology potentials with newly perceived consumer goods opportunities. Particular aspects of such needs, as portrayed by Vernon in his original US case,[2] were for products that could target the high-income consumers that were most willing and able to experiment with path-breaking and prestigious new goods. A notable characteristic of such items was that they could then be labour-saving in consumers' every day usage.

Vernon's detailed analysis of the innovation process itself gained separate influence and, as we will see, several aspects of it retained significant importance within the refocusing of emphasis from centralised to decentralised knowledge seeking (KS) and creative activity in MNEs (Chapter 7). Nevertheless, the way that Vernon positioned it in the original PLCM can now seem a challenging and somewhat idiosyncratic one. Having decisively emphasised how the objective of the innovation process would be the US *market* he felt the need to also articulate a separate logic for the initiation of *production* there. The theoretical alternative could have been the location of pioneering supply in a lower-cost overseas facility, whose initial output would be exclusively exported back to the US.[3] It is particular factors endemic to the needs of successful innovation that Vernon sees as precluding logical consideration of this trade-based supply alternative at this stage. We outline three of them here.

Firstly, it is indicated that successful innovation would require high-quality, often spontaneous and informal, exploratory communication between the separate vital functions ingrained in the process. Thus, the effective development of a major innovation will require inputs from market research (discerning and articulating a potentially high-value gap in the market), scientists (creating, and/or accessing externally, relevant new technologies), engineers (to put in place the prototype operable supply process) and top-level strategic management (to oversee, motivate and coordinate the whole effort). The intense, but often unpredictable, need for these functions to ask each other questions and, perhaps, to generate serendipitously potential new lines of exploratory investigation will, it is argued, benefit enormously from the co-location of the major players in the functional groups. Casual and ad hoc conversations may turn out to be as challenging and rewarding as pre-planned formal sessions. To project this core insight onto Vernon's specific question; the market research needs to be organised in the US (the accepted target market); the scientist needs to be there to tap into the high-quality (but only accessible) science-base; the strategic management are there by definition. If the engineers were mandated to operate elsewhere to formulate the prototype factory in response to a different (non-US) set of factor prices a number of these vital inter-functional communication exchanges would be damagingly compromised.

The second important feature of an innovation process is that it is likely to be iterative and gradualist. Though eventual success may be ensured by the sheer originality and obvious breakthrough value of the new good the precise form in which it will secure its mature and settled position in the market may take time to formalise. Early consumer feedback, though basically supportive, may recommend changes in important details of the offering, some elements of simplification, perhaps, or enhancement or refinement of other functions. But such revisions to the product characteristics may then require significant changes in the mix of relevant technologies; retaining the need for mutually exploratory inter-functional exchanges. This, in turn, may impose quite fundamental rethinking of the initial production technology. Where this results in changes in the input needs a location whose factor proportions and prices seemed optimal for the pioneering factory may become ineffective and high cost, so that an alternative location may now seem preferable. In this context any attempt to optimise a production location until the wider innovation formatting is complete is likely to be costly and destabilising. At this stage the engineering function operates in a context of bounded rationality, so that the operatively logical outcome would be to locate it alongside the other functions that it needs to respond to and interact with.

The third point regarding the nature of innovation as perceived by Vernon is that, given the assumptions about the market-driven context underpinning it, the price-elasticity of demand for the new goods will be low. These goods succeed with a high-income group of consumers because of their unique originality. Within reason price is not a leading or subtle influence within the decision process. If the acceptance of the need for home-country production of the newly innovated good does impose costs that are higher than they might have been elsewhere this is of little concern to the monopoly supplier, the costs can be passed on to the consumer.

At the completion of the PLCM's first stage two propositions are asserted which will feed into the firm's evolution in the stage to come. Firstly, the innovation process is considered to be finalised. Though the product will be routinely subject to evolution within the normal processes of market-responsive competitive dynamics it has reached maturity; the more basic exploration of its nature is now fulfilled and its positioning understood. Secondly, however, this market positioning is still perceived, in the light of the innovation itself, to be entirely domestic. The firm has no international connections or, as yet, ambitions.

THE MATURE PRODUCT STAGE

The central theme of the second stage of the PLCM is that of the firm's internationalisation and the start of its metamorphosis to a fully articulated MNE. Once the unquestioned success of the innovation stage is decisively asserted, in the form of a large and increasingly visible and influential domestic market for the new good, intuitive forces begin to underline the plausibility and competitive logic of this second stage.

The first, very ad hoc, signs of this process were seen to emerge in the form of small amounts of demand for the new US goods in some relatively prosperous foreign markets. Initially this would have been organised and transacted by independent trade agents, with no systematic involvement of the firms. However, as the income levels in such foreign economies become increasingly closer to that of the US when the good was innovated there, these markets impinged more systematically on the firm's planning for its own evolution. An initial step would have been to take internalised responsibility for the growth of these exports by establishing its own marketing and distribution operations in key overseas markets.[4] In fact this interpretation reflected two new approaches to explaining trade patterns that were emerging in the early 1960s. Firstly, it could be seen as 'technology gap' trade (Posner, 1961; Hufbauer, 1966, 23–34), where exports reflect the originality and technological superiority of the newly innovated goods, rather than a cost-based ability to produce standardised mass-market goods competitively. Secondly, the trade derives from specific characteristics of the products and their relevance to the *demand* structures of particular foreign markets – again rather than reflecting current *supply* conditions. Thus it reflects the concept of taste overlaps postulated in the theorising of Burenstam-Linder (1961). Significantly, however, from the perspective of IB thinking, these characteristics, being a distinctive technology-based competitiveness embodied in products that are generating demand in foreign markets, are precisely our OAs.[5] The crucial next step addressed by Vernon in this stage of the PLCM is when and why it becomes strategically viable to apply these OAs in overseas production instead of exporting.

Vernon offers two types of explanation for the FDI decision in the context of these new goods asserting their position in other high-income markets. The first is essentially an application of a conventional cost-of-supply calculus. Thus 'the marginal costs of producing for export in the home unit plus international transport costs and duties are compared with the full costs of producing the required amount in a foreign subsidiary' (Vernon, 1979, 257). Two types of cost are implicit in this formulation, with both being routinely dependent on a large enough local market to realise the supply potential. Firstly, input costs may be to some degree lower than in the home country. Given the implied similarity in income levels, however, such differences are likely to be relatively small and unlikely to be a front-line consideration. Thus, it is the second factor, tariff and transport costs, which we can now see as having more influence. The competitive benefits of avoiding these costs can now be classified as 'tariff jumping' market-seeking (MS) FDI. This may, however, be interpreted as 'defensive' behaviour by the firm. Barring such major input cost differences its preference might, in terms of this cost calculus, have remained home-country production (benefitting from familiar conditions) and export.

The second explanation for the initiation of production in the target market is more 'positive', in the sense of involving an important element of proactive strategic responsiveness very early in the life of the firm as an MNE. Inevitably, any firm that has brought a major innovation to market, by effectively extending the scope of its industry in decisive and path-breaking ways, will expect to soon face competition from rival products aiming to provide alternative variants of the core breakthrough service. This scenario takes on distinctive facets in the case of a foreign market initially developed by imports from the original innovating firm. Here it may be local enterprises that seek to emerge as the first 'challenger' suppliers. They will have strengths and weaknesses in aiming to do this. As insurgents attempting to design around the central technologies possessed by the now mature incumbents (their OA) these putative entrants will inevitably be at a disadvantage. Against this the original innovators will have provided them with a clear target, by already having (at notable expense over considerable time) put in place a clear understanding of the basic new service that consumers now expect. It is here that the local firm may find an immediate advantage. In completing the formulation of its own product variant it will, of necessity, respond as fully as possible to the distinctive characteristics of local demand patterns. This may then expose vulnerabilities in the imported goods. The iterative original innovation process of these goods will have settled on formats precisely reflecting the needs of the consumers of the originating country (for example, US) and these may differ significantly from those of the new target market (for example, Europe). Whilst the sheer unique originality of the good will attract significant demand for the exported good, 'host-country' consumers may nevertheless have viewed its 'home-country' details with considerable reservations. Responding to these taste differences in the formulation of their rival variants should be an immediate source of advantage achieved by incipient local producers compared to the perceived limitations of the imports. But if the original innovator then switches its mode of supply from trade to local production it has the means to overcome this, by adapting the details of its product to respond to these local taste idiosyncrasies. Indeed, its experience of the practice of such adaptation during the iterative redesign stages of the original innovation will have inculcated an ability and willingness to address such responsiveness.

This interpretation would suggest an important internationalising consciousness in the behaviour of these firms, even in the very early stages of their emergence as MNEs. The implied decision processes would indicate an awareness of the future importance of international perspectives in their competitive development as firms. The proto-FDI decisions intuit strategic implications, rather than simply optimising the rent-seeking capacities of current scopes and markets. Two aspects of *responsiveness* are implied. Firstly, market responsiveness where the firms, even after completion of the core innovation, retain an awareness of evolving market conditions; both through *time* (changes in an individual market) and across *space* (reacting to different tastes in a newly entered foreign market). Secondly, competitive responsiveness through an awareness of rivals' moves and potentials. This early stage scenario thus projects entry into foreign-market production as a strategically reactive response to local-firms' threat to an established export position. Once the emerging MNE positioned itself in a number of foreign markets in this way it will become (in a way we will elaborate in the next chapter) a *multi-domestic hierarchy*, applying a responsive MS approach to competing in a range of separate foreign economies.

THE STANDARDISED PRODUCT STAGE

If a key implicit insight of the mature product stage of the PLCM was of internationalisation as a reactive strategic move aimed at slowing down the emergence of rival firms challenging the innovator's hegemony then it becomes a core premise of Vernon's final stage that this battle will eventually be lost. Eventually, the good becomes sufficiently standardised for there to be mass markets in a wide range of countries for, at least, its more basic variants. In the process of the growth of such standardised and mainly simplified versions of the product the main technologies will have become much more widely accessible so that many more firms will have been able to enter the industry. Thus, the mode of competition relating to these goods has moved from the monopoly supply of a new luxury innovation, or even the subsequent emphasis on its product differentiation and marketing, to a decisive basis in price. From the point where price-*in*elasticity during the product development stage could isolate the innovation from cost concerns a very high price-elasticity will now impose the need to seek out low-cost production locations for the standardised product.

Alongside the incipient lowering of trade barriers on these types of goods[6] the growth of extensive globalised markets for such standardised goods would refocus MNEs' location choice from the demand characteristics of host countries to their supply-side input potentials. This element of their global strategy would now seek to separate where a product was produced from where it would be sold. The MS FDI of the mature product stage is now replaced by an efficiency-seeking (ES) motivation. In terms of future IB theorising the negative LAs of developed country MS (restraints on trade) is now superseded by the positive LAs of (usually) developing countries (low-cost inputs).

Vernon's own first (1966) exposition of such standardised product stage characteristics was predominantly one of speculation and prediction. Here he prefaces his most precise expression of the possibility of such ES-supply behaviour by suggesting (1966, 204) that it would be difficult to think 'of many cases in which manufacturers of standardised products in the more advanced countries had made significant investments in the less-developed countries with a view of exporting such products from these countries'.

The predictive value of this was, however, we now know, on the verge of being comprehensively validated. Also essentially accurate was his suggestion that 'the low cost of labour may be the initial attraction drawing the investor to less-developed areas' (ibid., 203).[7] In terms of the formulations to be expounded in the next chapter such a movement from a mainly MS subsidiary imperative to an ES-supply-based emphasis represents an MNE's organisational structure evolving from a multi-domestic hierarchy to a network hierarchy.

THE SELF-OBSOLESCING PLCM

In Vernon's own (1979, 265) subsequent evaluation the original PLCM 'had strong predictive power in the first two or three decades after World War II, especially in explaining the composition of US trade and in projecting the likely patterns of foreign direct investment by US firms'. Furthermore, as will be frequently referenced here, individual facets of the framework remained significantly relevant to subsequent developments in thinking about IB and the MNE. However, it quite quickly became clear that changes in the competitive environment and in the scope and ambitions of the firms were undermining the logic of the PLCM as a sequential formulation. Of the two changes we can emphasise here one was essentially external to the firms, but the other was not only endogenous to them but also clearly implied within the logic of the PLCM itself.

The background to the original PLCM assumed the innovation of very distinctive products in the US, then a uniquely high-income market. These goods would then, somewhat later, become of relevance to other countries (for example, in Europe) when they had attained levels of prosperity similar to those that had prevailed in the US when initially marketed there. But by the late 1970s a significant number of these other economies had secured current income levels closely comparable to that of the US. The gradualist scenario in which demand for a new good slowly emerged in a foreign market and eventually led to local production became competitively redundant. A new innovation, even if still initially secured entirely in the home country, needed to be got into now competitively significant foreign markets not only *quickly* but also, as our interpretation of the second stage of the PLCM already told us, in ways *responsive* to these markets' distinctive characteristics and needs.

But the second change precisely addresses this challenge. The establishment of MS production and marketing subsidiaries in these countries provides an in-place, and presumably enthusiastic, vehicle to secure this objective. Once a major new innovation is clearly asserting its success in the home country such well-managed MS subsidiaries, successfully embedded in their host economy, will surely lobby aggressively for the right to take on its responsive and adaptive supply for their own market. This suggests the collapse of the first two stages of the original PLCM into one internationally differentiated innovation process; still initially centralised but very promptly diffusing into a set of dispersed market-responsive variants.

This can now, however, be seen as a harbinger of a much more fundamental change in the competitive organisation of MNEs: the decentralisation of innovation itself and the embracing of a KS motivation at the subsidiary level. Thus, once subsidiaries in the more advanced economies began to see themselves as increasingly proactive vehicles for the exploitation of centralised innovation, the most ambitious of them would begin to compare the innovation-oriented creative capacities of their hosts as comparable, but also potentially distinctively different, to those of the home country. It would become viable for them to assert themselves as sources of innovation, reflecting unique competences of their host economy but providing new goods with international potentials for the parent MNE group. The varied aspects of these new KS horizons (as embodied, for example, in the heterarchical or transnational organisation structures) will become the central focus of Chapter 7.

NOTES

1. Probably the first significantly influential introduction to Hymer's work was in Kindleberger (1969).
2. Later Vernon (1979, 256) extended such characteristics to suggest that innovations by Continental European firms could be material-saving and capital-saving, whilst Japanese firms would seek to conserve space, as well as materials and capital, in their innovations.
3. One reason for Vernon's perceived need to address this, at the time counter-intuitive and counterfactual, possibility may simply have been his preoccupation with trade behaviour in motivating his study.
4. Within the scope of our definition this would be where the firm becomes an MNE, since even these marketing and/or distribution operations represent overseas value-added activities.
5. Vernon himself soon came to adopt this mode of thinking. Thus the PLCM suggests that 'firms that set up foreign producing facilities characteristically do so in reliance on some real or imagined monopolistic advantage [which allows them] to take on the special costs and uncertainties of operating a subsidiary in a foreign environment' (Vernon, 1979, 255–6). An 'innovation lead' is then 'one such special strength'.
6. Early tariff cuts were most significant on the types of goods that developed and middle-income economies were likely to want to import but be much less likely to seek to produce competitively.
7. This did not imply, of course, that the processes of technological standardisation at this stage of the PLCM involved a dominant or systematic tendency towards the use of unskilled labour. Rather it implied that the internationalised perspectives of these

firms *as* MNEs meant that where large quantities of unskilled labour *were* needed these companies could benefit competitively from relocating these elements of their activity to less-developed economies. One aspect of this was that the MNEs could raise the capital for such ES operations on relatively low-cost international markets and thereby overcome a possible constraint of high-cost capital in low-income economies.

4. From multi-domestic hierarchy to network hierarchy

INTRODUCTION

In the previous chapter we showed how Vernon's analysis, though setting out with very different objectives, reinforced Hymer's perception of the need to understand the MNE as a significant economic influence and also put into place very important insights that projected forward to major roles in future IB theorising. We also noted, in passing, how Vernon's discussion also carried precise implications regarding the organisational forms the MNE could take and how these would reflect their need to address different and changing strategic objectives. In this chapter we build on these insights by introducing the multi-domestic hierarchy (MH) as the prevailing MNE structure of the mid-1960s (achieved in Vernon's analysis as the culmination of an internationalising firm's 'mature product' stage) and then tracing how the competitive forces of incipient globalisation required its transition to network hierarchy (NH) (implicit in Vernon's 'standardised product' stage).

MULTI-DOMESTIC HIERARCHY

To understand and evaluate any organisational structure adopted by an MNE we need to ask two overarching questions. First of all, *how* can an originally national firm expand its value-adding operations into overseas locations; what are the sources of the competitiveness that allows it to do this? Next, *why* has it adopted the particular configuration of its overseas operations that prevails at a given time; what factors draw it into specific overseas commitments and what particular strategic imperatives are being addressed?

For the MH the pioneering analysis had already provided cogent answers to the first question. Hymer had shown how a putative MNE would need to own and control uniquely distinctive sources of firm-level competitive advantages, whilst Vernon had put detail into how these OA would be created in forms that reflected the firm's home-country environment but then also conditioned the types of overseas countries they were likely to aspire to enter. This leads us into the second question where the answer for MH MNEs was that they will have had operations in overseas economies whose *markets* quite closely resembled those of the home country and where external constraints determined a logic to *production* there. The MH was, in effect, a portfolio of independent self-contained MS operations.

Two institutional and policy-based contexts can be separated in determining the extensive growth of MS FDI in the two decades after 1945. Initially, in the already developed and industrialised economies. Here, though the MH's MS posture in these countries is now perceived as essentially negative and defensive, we can find two more dynamic and positive elements in the scenario. Firstly, these still protected and, by future standards, isolated economies were achieving very much improved levels of growth due to the implementation of Keynesian macro policies. Secondly, the MNEs themselves were becoming significantly more ambitious as they achieved increasingly successful programmes of innovation (enhanced OA) and accepted the need to address international markets to adequately achieve their full realisation. It was, therefore, the persistence of various barriers to trade (as 'negative' LAs) that determined the predominant activation of these evolving sources of international competitiveness through the MS strategies of the MH.

The second, quite differently originated, context relevant here was the implementation, most visibly in the 1950s in South America, of import-substitution strategies. Here the policy put up significant trade restraints on industrial goods already imported in significant quantities, with the aim of thereby creating an impetus to the domestic supply of these goods and the emergence of a localised industrial sector. The firms that had been supplying these markets through trade thus became the most plausible (though by no means uniquely or specifically targeted) candidates to implement this production; an MS investment pursuing 'tariff jumping' FDI.

Figure 4.1 provides a stylised presentation of an MH organisational structure. Here four MS subsidiaries are depicted as competing exclusively for the domestic market of their host economy. Possible rivals in this competition may be local enterprises or subsidiaries of other MNEs but not, by assumption, imports. By the same token the dominant trade-restrained context means that such MS subsidiaries have no logical diversion from fighting the most effective battle for their domestic market. From this it follows that, though locating the dominant conditioning factor in trade restraints points to the traditional 'tariff jumping' variant of MS, a degree of subsidiary-specific localising competitiveness can inculcate a clear element of local responsiveness as a differentiating MS strategic posture.

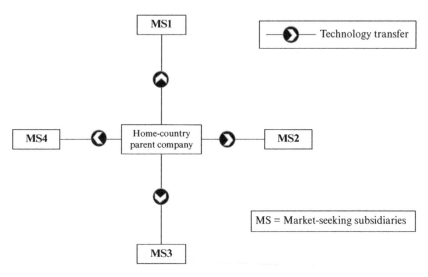

Figure 4.1   The multi-domestic hierarchy

This allows scope for managerial initiative in MS subsidiaries to encourage its marketing and engineering groups, and provide technological discretion where needed in order to adapt the inherited group products to local tastes and production conditions. This, however, it needs to be emphasised, would be entirely tactical. Any adaptations achieved will be precise responses to distinctive aspects of their unique domestic competitive environment and not expected to be transferable. Other MS subsidiaries in the multi-domestic portfolio will address their own adaptive needs in their own way.

These latter points take us to the decisively *hierarchical* nature of the MH. Despite the allowance for certain degrees of responsive flexibility the existence of an MS subsidiary is totally subservient to the home-country parent company. The original establishment of the subsidiary would have been based on centrally created and controlled sources of competitiveness and its survival will always be dependent on the authorisation and support of the clearly defined parent company. Thus the major dimensions of the hierarchical power exercised by the parent company in the MH are to decide where MS subsidiaries represent viable propositions and the extent of the group's current product scope that any such operation can usefully be authorised to supply there. As the figure shows, this limits logically systemic intra-group transactions to transfers of knowledge from the parent to each MS subsidiary. The content of these technology transfers is likely to vary according to the perceived local-market possibilities open to each subsidiary. Some defining core products of the MNE may be allocated to virtually all of the subsidiaries, whilst other more specialised or niche goods may be seen as relevant to only selected MS operations.

In our interpretation there were major inefficiencies endemic to these MS multi-domestic strategies that would soon be exposed by revitalised competitiveness in the global economy and gradually provoke the first major restructuring of the post-war MNEs. In the MH the success of an MNE group comprises the aggregated success of separate subsidiaries. For each of these MS facilities this will be determined by the potential of its local market and how well it is able to realise this. Here we can draw out three potential sources of subsidiary-level inefficiencies that reflect aspects of the MS context. The most obvious of these would be the limited size of the market to which the subsidiary is constrained. It may often need to operate below its optimal scale of production and, therefore, not be able to realise the target level of productive efficiency.

Equally implicit in the very nature of the MS strategy is the second endemic source of subsidiary-level inefficiency; that of 'inappropriate technology transfer'. The key determinant of which parts of an MNE's current product range are selected for supply by an MS subsidiary is, of course, the perceived needs of its local consumers. It is host-country demand conditions that define the subsidiary's output profile. However, these goods were developed in the MNE's home country, and their successful and accepted production technologies were refined in reflection of that country's input characteristics. But the defining characteristics of the new host-country's production environment may be very different. This will often imply that the MS subsidiary finds itself using large quantities of more expensive local inputs, whilst unable to benefit from the use of those more readily available and lower-cost inputs that define the country's natural source of comparative advantage. This can be a major source of cost-inefficiency in its production. Though good subsidiary management and engineering may aspire to a certain degree of adaptation, it is unlikely to have the capacity (or parent company permission) to significantly change the core of basically proven and successful technologies.

The most stridently visible policy failure attributable to inappropriate technology transfer was that of the import-substitution industrialisation strategy adopted by many developing countries in the 1950s. Here the goods targeted for localised production were ones already imported by a relatively prosperous cosmopolitan elite familiar with developed economy consumer standards. Once again, alongside the relatively small size of such markets, the implied production technologies applied by MNEs, as major players in implementing localised supply, were fundamentally out of line with the developing country's logical input potentials. But here the implications went far beyond inefficiencies in production since the policy fundamentally subverted its developmental objectives. Firstly, by significantly building on and enhancing imbalances and inequalities in the economy, reinforcing dominant urban/rural and industrial/agricultural dualisms. Secondly, by considerably neglecting the real sources of the country's comparative advantage and marginalising sectors with genuine indigenous potentials that could have realised them.

The third compromising force likely to be built into the MS mode of operation is that of X-inefficiency. Here the subsidiary's influential personnel (top managers; marketing groups; engineers) may simply fail to fully realise the competitive potentials of the OA provided to them. One aspect of this is that they simply may not bother to address the issues of localised adaptation (product and/or process) that, whilst tactical rather than strategic, may have real competitive relevance. This, in turn, reflects a limitation of the MH as an international organisational structure. Because each MS subsidiary is fighting its own unique competitive battle informed means of assessing its true performance (actual relative to potential) may be quite opaque to the parent. It is a context of limited information (each subsidiary can claim to understand the potentials and problems of its host economy more fully than the parent could aspire to) and of bounded rationality decision making. Ultimately, each subsidiary may be evaluated in terms of the perceived adequacy of its ability to return profits, or assert growth potentials, to the parent.

At this point in our narrative we need to bring together our IB theory and business strategy themes to address a now obvious question. If the MH organisation and its MS subsidiaries were so complicit in acceptance of productive inefficiencies how had they been able to persist for so long? The answer we can offer is that the ability of the subsidiary to earn sufficient profits to satisfy the parent company derived not from achievement of productive efficiency but from the exercise of market power. Our analysis points towards two sources of this. Firstly, the strengths of the OAs that the subsidiary inherits from its parent company allow it to assert a market-leading position *within* its host country. Secondly, that country's 'negative' LAs, in the form of restraints on trade, protect the subsidiary from *external* challenges in the form of goods produced more efficiently elsewhere. But, moving into the last third of the twentieth century, we can find changes emerging which undermined these bases of the subsidiary-level introversion that defined the MH and begin the generation of a much more intensive *globalised* context for MNE competitiveness.

The main institutional and policy changes that began to emerge and challenge the viability of the MH as the MNEs' most logical organisational form were declines in protectionism and moves towards freer trade. The multilateral flagship of this was the completion of the Kennedy round of trade negotiations under the auspices of the General Agreement on Tariffs and Trade (GATT). Alongside this the implementation of integration in Europe was also becoming visible by the mid-1960s. Also, and perhaps most directly indicative of the types of restructuring that MNEs would need to embrace, was the abandonment of import-substitution industrialisation policies by many of its pioneering adherents and its replacement by carefully articulated export-oriented strategies based around these countries' sources of natural comparative advantage. It is then pertinent to note that the theoretical advocacy for these policies within mainstream economics placed decisive emphasis on their capacity to improve productive efficiency. What this same body of theorising was unaware of was that a major agent in securing such efficiency gains would be reactive competitive restructuring within MNEs. In the same way it took some time before trade analysis recognised that not only did MNEs play a major role in the growth in trade but also that a significant proportion of that was actually intra-group trade *within* MNEs.

The second change that intensified global competitiveness and challenged the established modes of IB behaviour was the emergence of many new MNEs from an increasing range of home countries. This then undermined the hegemonic competitive status of incumbent firms by diluting the market power they could exercise through their so-far-dominant OAs. The new firms not only added many more OAs to the international market place but also often brought distinctive new dimensions to them. Our long-term perspective on the development of IB will then find two specific new challenges to MNEs. Inevitably, it will point to the increasingly intense need for all MNEs (new and old) to renew and revitalise their OAs and, eventually, to do this internationally; that is, *as* MNEs. As knowledge seeking we will discuss this progression in Chapter 7. The more immediately perceived challenge, however, was to optimise the performance (profitability; growth; market share) that they could get from their already fully realised in-place OAs. For a well-established MH this would require major restructuring to eliminate the endemic inefficiencies of MS subsidiaries and to replace it with an efficiency-seeking (ES) orientation. It should be observed, however, that many of the newer MNEs were based, *ab initio*, around a cost-competitive positioning in a freer-market global economy. As we will elaborate in our discussion of the work of Kojima (1978; see Chapter 5 here) the 'first wave' of Japanese FDI, into other Southeast Asian economies, exemplified this cost-competitive MNE strategy and was classified (within trade theoretic concerns) as 'trade creating'.

In our stylised narrative of MNEs' strategic evolution we now have the basis for their restructuring from the MS MH to the ES *network hierarchy* (NH).

NETWORK HIERARCHY (NH)

We have interpreted the emergence of the NH as being integral to the forces that led to intensified global competition in the later decades of the twentieth century. This meant that many of the MNEs that took their first steps into international activity as a response to the potentials and challenges of these new conditions did so in immediate conformity with the dictates of the NH format. Nevertheless, to most fully demonstrate the nature of NH and how it reflected specific evolutionary facets of the wider economic change, we will focus here on its logic as an internal evolution from the MH.

We observe three potentials in the repositioning of individual subsidiaries as MNEs move from MH towards NH. Firstly, the closure of established MS facilities. The source of such a possibility would be that a high-income developed market providing considerable demand-side attractions to an MNE would be less likely to possess the supply-side capacities to attract cost-competitive production of any of the firm's major products. Its level of development implies an inherently high-cost structure for relevant inputs. This, in fact, provides a very clear exemplification of the types of inappropriate technology transfer that compromised efficiency in MS subsidiaries. Nevertheless, the wider competitive parameters of such an evolving MNE may still seek to find these subsidiaries some form of surviving role, beyond the pure dictates of ES. The country's market still remains a vital one, albeit one the group would prefer to supply through imports. The likely bad publicity of the high-profile closure of an important operation might severely compromise its persistence in the market, alienating both consumers and the government and its agencies. An alternative might then be more forward looking, involving increased access to the creative talents available in such an economy and presaging the types of KS product-development strategies soon to emerge more forcefully in leading MNEs.

The second restructuring possibility would be the setting up of new ES-supply bases in less-developed low-cost economies whose limited demand potentials had excluded any previous MS facilities. This would be very much compatible with the type of export-oriented industrialisation strategy many such countries were moving towards. In line with the standardised product stage of Vernon's PLCM it would show MNEs turning the potentials of freer trade to their advantage and thereby allowing such countries to activate their neglected sources of comparative advantage. Thus we see the ES emphasis here as targeting a host-country's *positive* LAs (internationally competitive supply inputs) instead of the defensive reaction to *negative* LAs (trade restraints) in the MS motivation. It also now involves *appropriate* technology transfer.

The intermediate, but by no means compromise, third possibility would be to restructure a subsidiary from an earlier MS emphasis towards an ES role. This would involve the abandonment of a large part of its previous local-market product range (now to be supplied through trade from a more efficient operation elsewhere) and to focus on a small range of goods that local input conditions will allow it to supply effectively. Though this will now narrow the *subsidiary's* local commitment to the functionally limited manufacture of a small number of products for the export market the MNE would be likely to retain an acceptably high profile through its (possibly separate) marketing operations covering a much more extensive range of the group's products.

We can now see how the transition to ES as the dominant subsidiary motivation in the NH can overcome each of the three sources of productive inefficiency we attributed to the MH structure. With access to the group's international markets an ES subsidiary should be able to fully achieve economies of scale in producing its goods. Informed and careful selection of the most efficient location for each good would remove the potential for inappropriate technology to inflate production costs. Lastly, the fact that each subsidiary's position in the group is, to some degree, always provisional and conditional should eliminate any persistent X-inefficiency precisely because, as the aim of the ES global-supply network is to maximise the group's cost-competitiveness for external markets, it will also become internally competitive. Individual subsidiaries would always need to be ready to make the efficiency-based case for accession to new supply responsibilities and at the same time to defend their entitlement to their current ones.

In the NH the hierarchical power and interventionist responsibility of the parent HQ becomes considerably enhanced relative to that needed in the MH. The HQ will now not only determine which subsidiaries have a role to play but also a much more persistent involvement in how they play it. Its influence extends over both how subsidiaries exercise their immediate responsibilities and also the assessment of how these responsibilities may evolve over time in the group's context. Thus, in the short run, the HQ needs to oversee the effective realisation of the group's current competitive potential. It needs to secure the maximum international demand for the current range of products and ensure that effective communication mechanisms lead to the relevant production units supplying them through well-coordinated intra-group trade. As Figure 4.2 shows, in the NH each supply facility can be exporting to many markets, whilst an (often separate) local marketing group imports and distributes other parts of the range.

But into the longer term the HQ has to handle the innate dynamics of such an NH; the static optimising implications of efficiency maximisation

The development of international business

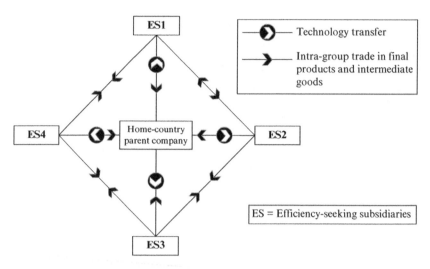

Figure 4.2   The network hierarchy

do not, in practice, override inevitable forces of change. If, as would have been hoped, the participation of MNEs' ES subsidiaries in export-oriented development strategies led to successful growth this would change the relevant input characteristics. From an IB theory perspective development implies changing LAs. Though this may lead to higher input costs (for example, wage rates) this may be accompanied by more-than-matching improvements in efficiency (for example, higher productivity in labour; more reliable energy supply; better infrastructure). Responding to these upgrading changes as positive potentials the HQ will be always be open to reconfiguring the supply network; not closing ES units in a 'footloose' manner but allocating to a subsidiary new higher-value-added supply responsibilities that reflect enhanced potentials. Where this occurs it will require new (and newly appropriate) technology transfers from the parent to subsidiaries. Figure 4.2 again shows the only knowledge transfers in the group as from the home country to subsidiaries. Here, by comparison with MH, the content of these transfers are much more selective, restricted to those relevant to the subsidiary's allocated supply responsibilities.

There is then another aspect of this latter point, again relating to the parent company's persisting hierarchical status. Though the group's expectations of its overseas operations are still constrained to the objective of efficient supply of its current products, the centre will be fully aware of the need to consistently add to this range through its commitment to product development. But once the home-country operation has successfully completed an innovation the intensified pressures of globalised competition will lead it to quickly consider the potentials of cost-cutting relocation of supply to an ES unit somewhere in its network. Selection of the most suitable subsidiary to accede to this role is another of the most dynamic hierarchical responsibilities of the HQ, built around the persistence and renewal of 'outward' technology transfer.

5. Trade and FDI revisited: the role of location

INTRODUCTION

Although it was far from his intention to do so, the work of Kojima (1973, 1978, 1982) elaborated on the relationship between trade and FDI in ways that also provided a challengingly different organising context for some of the key insights that were emerging in the firm-level theorising on the MNE. The focus of Kojima's exposition was to delineate the different circumstances that would determine whether FDI was a substitute for trade or a complement to it. From this he was also able to point towards the relationship between types of FDI and important normative issues in economics. His approach to this was based on elucidation of observed real-world cases interpreted through the macro-level methodologies of mainstream international economics. In adopting this approach he did not wish to address the ways that available micro-level IB insights on the firms that were doing the FDI could interface very precisely with the behaviour he sought to explain and evaluate. He thus foregoes the explanatory power of the contingent influence of different types of recipient country LAs and how this determined the different MNE strategic objectives that, in effect, were central to the FDI scenarios he draws out.

From this background in trade theory and motivated by precise normative or evaluative concerns Kojima therefore built his analysis around two stylised cases which are then exemplified in the interpretation of real-world cases. Here it is the case of trade-oriented or trade-creating FDI (TC/ FDI) that exemplifies his prescriptive advocacy for the conditions where FDI can generate normative benefits in terms of enhanced efficiency and positive dynamic effects in the international economy. Then, he suggests, FDI *should* flow from the investing country's most comparatively disadvantaged (competitively marginal) industry and into host countries where the industry does not exist but has a clear potential to do so; it has a *latent* comparative advantage there. As we will elaborate, Kojima's template for this was the 'first wave' of Japanese FDI into, at that stage, underdeveloped economies in Southeast Asia. We will also elaborate how, in the IB terms excluded by Kojima, the FDI embodies OAs that serve to complement unrealised positive LAs in the host countries in ways that enhance static resource efficiency in production and provide a major dynamic impetus to these countries' development.

In Kojima's alternative scenario the FDI flows *from* an industry that remains amongst its country's most comparatively advantaged, and is not showing any major signs of competitive vulnerability, and *into* another country where the industry also exists though at a presumed lower level of productive efficiency. The trade theoretic prescription would be that the foreign market (in the FDI's host country) would have been most effectively supplied through trade. The FDI is thus, for Kojima, trade destroying (TD/FDI), and by diverting production from a more efficient to a less efficient location it is compromising to effective resource allocation. It was exemplified by US FDI into Europe in the immediate post-war decades and made FDI complicit in the inherent inefficiencies of the persisting protectionist environment. In IB terms it was thus predominantly 'tariff jumping' MS investment responding to the negative LAs of trade restraints.

TRADE-CREATING FOREIGN DIRECT INVESTMENT (TC/FDI)

In a stylised presentation of the TC/FDI case the source of the FDI is the least comparatively advantaged industry of its home country (C1), so that its precise aim is to alleviate this revealed competitive vulnerability. In pursuit of this objective the FDI will flow into a host country (C2) where the industry does not yet exist but is perceived to have a clear potential to do so. Thus, in C2, the underlying conditions for efficient production of the industry's goods already exist (a latent or potential comparative advantage) but some developmental bottleneck has prevented this from occurring. In Kojima's exposition the transferable FDI package from C1 takes relevant complementary (industry-defining) factors (technology, managerial skills, market access) to C2. This then allows the initiation of production in C2, which will embody, and thus bring into hopefully internationally competitive activation, the previously latent sources of comparative advantage. In Figure 5.1 we depict the refocusing of trade patterns from this relocation of production.

Before the FDI the industry's production is centralised in the developed economy C1. Since the host country C2 is assumed to be a low-income developing economy its demand for the output of the industry is small and met by limited exports from C1. Here ROW (rest of the world) represents all other economies likely to provide a market for the industry's goods. But C1's exports to ROW will again be limited because of its

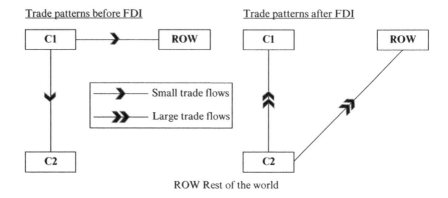

Figure 5.1   Trade-creating foreign direct investment (FDI)

marginal competitiveness in the industry. Once the industry has effectively relocated its supply to C2 the highly cost-efficient production there will alter trade patterns. The limited demand for the good in C2 will now be met locally and, more significantly, exports from C2 will now supply the home-country C1 market that would have previously relied on inefficient domestic production; trade between C1 and C2 reverses in direction and expands greatly. Demand in ROW is now met by exports from C2 rather than C1, and again expands considerably as the supply source is now more competitive. In fact because production is now much more cost-efficient, the demand in C1 and ROW is not only supplied more competitively but is also likely to be expanded overall. It is, for Kojima, clearly 'trade-creating' FDI that provides the benefits of free-trade that allows the realisation of countries' sources of comparative advantage.

We can see three potential beneficiaries from this TC/FDI scenario. Firstly *consumers*, who in C1, C2 and ROW should all become better off. This comes not just from established customers getting the good at a more competitive price but also from extending demand to people who could not afford it before. Secondly, the C1 *industry* has revitalised its efficiency and competitiveness. Thirdly, there are benefits at the *country* level. This is decisively clear for C2, which has now received a vital impetus to growth and development from highly productive activation of its sources of comparative advantage. For C1 the potential benefits are more contingent but clearly there. Here, in the presence of an effective structural adjustment mechanism, resources that are released from a comparatively disadvantaged industry through outward FDI would be quickly and efficiently redeployed, at higher productivity levels, in expanding (probably recently emergent) industries that are manifesting new sources of comparative advantage. This would upgrade C1's industrial sector towards higher-value-added competitiveness that would also provide new sources of exports.

However, there is an important question left unresolved by Kojima's exposition. It tells us convincingly *when* and *why* such TC/FDI should occur, but not *how*. How is it that C1's most comparatively *dis*advantaged industry, its most competitively weak and vulnerable, can undertake something recognised to be as difficult and challenging as FDI? From an IB perspective we can resolve this conundrum in ways that enrich the scope of the analysis whilst retaining the prescriptive insights of Kojima's model. Here we separate two sources of competitiveness for a national industry. Firstly, the sources of firm-specific competitive advantages that basically define the industry's distinctive nature (our OAs). Secondly, the ability of the country to supply the relevant inputs to the firms' processes at competitive prices (LAs, in the form of labour of various skills, energy, raw materials and so on).

We can now see that the source of the loss of competitiveness that emerges in C1 reflects declining efficiency of the relevant LAs (for example, higher wages; more expensive energy or raw materials) alongside OAs that still retain their industry-relevant effectiveness. Thus the *firms* move from C1 to C2 in pursuit of renewed sources of cost-effective inputs (our LAs), to replace those lost at home. These will then complement their OAs, which still retain their established competitive potency. We can thus recast Kojima's 'FDI package' as a firm-level organisational process that transfers relevant OAs to C2, so as to reconfigure there the OA-LA combination that had earlier been competitively efficient in C1. By working with the LAs that define the latent comparative advantage of C2, the C1 firms help overcome the 'developmental bottlenecks' there and activate its efficient growth as an internationally competitive economy.

Projecting these analytical perspectives on TC/FDI back onto the case from which Kojima derived them can again illustrate the value of a continued dialectic between the MNE and the real worlds it operates in and the theoretical structures aiming to interpret and evaluate it. Thus TC/FDI is exemplified by the 'first wave' of Japanese FDI into other Asian economies, notably those that would soon become characterised as the 'newly industrialised countries' (NICs). The industries and operations involved had achieved strong, export-oriented, competitiveness *in* Japan after World War II by using low-cost labour in conjunction with standardised labour-intensive technology to produce already successful mass-market consumer goods.[1] The emerging international competitiveness of these industries can be interpreted as based on two elements. Firstly, LAs in the form of low-cost labour, defining Japan's macro-level source of comparative advantage at that time. Secondly, the attributes (OAs) that emerged at the firm-level to give Japanese companies the ability to make effective use of these readily available LAs. These OAs took forms reflecting both the characteristics of the industries and of the national background (LAs) within which they were developed. Thus, at that stage, the Japanese companies' OAs included a strong mastery of the labour-intensive technology relevant to these industries; managerial expertise in organising large unskilled labour forces; skills in marketing standardised mass-market goods; access to worldwide networks so as to market and distribute large quantities of goods.

The sheer success of these industries in Japan ultimately led to rises in wage rates, thus removing the key LA (low labour costs) underpinning international competitiveness. The industries became disadvantaged in Japan; that is, they lost competitiveness, relative to those emerging higher-technology, more capital-intensive industries that could afford and utilise higher-cost but increasingly skilled labour. But the firms in these industries retained their OAs and believed they had more chance of sustaining their competitive survival by continuing to use these industry-specific attributes in familiar ways than by attempting to move to other industries in Japan. Thus they looked for new sources of low-cost labour abroad.[2]

In other Asian economies, in the 1960s, there were abundant sources of low-cost labour that were not being activated as an actual comparative advantage because local firms did not then possess the attributes (technology; organisational abilities; market access) to do so. The combination of the Japanese companies' OAs and the Asian countries' LAs therefore allowed the firms to continue to supply their existing markets cost effectively (perhaps more so), whilst the countries started a development process around revealed sources of comparative advantage. Complementary to this was the way Japan's policy-based industrial restructuring facilitated the absorption of the resources released as the declining industries relocated production through FDI into newly emergent and more technology- and skill-intensive sectors that provided preserved export competitiveness.[3]

TRADE-DESTROYING FOREIGN DIRECT INVESTMENT (TD/FDI)

Kojima models his TD/FDI as being from a comparatively advantaged industry in its home country (C3) into another relatively developed host country (C4), where the same industry does already exist. Characterising the status of the industry in C4 before the inflow of FDI, Kojima suggests it may or may not be comparatively advantaged relative to other industries in C4, but is assumed to be operating at an absolutely lower level of productivity than the industry in C3 (from which the FDI will come). So the best way for the industry in C3 to meet its (viably extensive) demand in C4 would be through exports. The FDI into C4 *may* improve the industry's efficiency there to some degree but, because there is no expectation (contrary to C2 in the TC/FDI case) of any significant sources of unrealised potential competitiveness there, it is assumed this will not be enough to raise supply in C4 to the level of efficiency that persists in C3. Thus, after the FDI, less efficient production in C4 replaces more effective production in C3 so that welfare is diminished. The FDI substitutes for trade and is, therefore, trade destroying.

Developing this case along the lines implied by Kojima's articulation we see that, where circumstances permit, the industry in C3 would find it most efficient and competitive to supply its share of the market in C4 through trade. Here, in the absence of FDI, trade would occur along the lines dictated by comparative advantage. Thus, when the FDI does occur, it needs to be attributed to factors that undermine this preference for trade. The most logical of these, within a basis in trade theory, would be the presence of trade barriers in C4. But, since the industry does already exist in C4, some more competitively dynamic reason for a closer local involvement there may also become relevant. Crucially, once the FDI has taken place, it will be substituting for trade; that is, TD/FDI.[4] By contrast with the TC/FDI case Kojima finds no room for beneficial structural adjustment in C3 following the TD/FDI; any such response would be perverse and illogical. The implication would be that resources released from industries with established international competitiveness were likely to become unemployed or reactivated in less efficient sectors. Any productivity improvements in C4 may support limited and routine growth, but not provide the radical dynamic developmental scope of the industry-initiating TC/FDI into C2.

Once again we can recast this narrative in IB terms. Here we see the industry in C3 as populated by firms with highly effective OAs and operating in an economy that is fully capable of complementing those OAs as an internationally competitive source of the relevant input LAs. The OAs provide the firms with the *ability* to carry out FDI, but the continuing access to strong LAs at home removes the *need* to do so. There is no positive efficiency-based incentive to FDI in C4 since the lower level of productivity there indicates that input LAs there may be less effective than in C3. That FDI by C3 firms in C4 does occur must, therefore, reflect forces disruptive to the continuation of cost-competitive, comparative-advantage-based trade. We can suggest two factors that have this effect. Firstly, still within the compass of trade theory is the presence of what we have called negative LAs in the form of tariff barriers or other artificial restraints on trade. Secondly, the firms may be developing more broadly based global-strategy approaches for the use and defence of their OAs. Then production in C4, although lowering immediate productive efficiency, may be seen to play a locally proactive competitive role. It does need to compete with other already viable firms in a market worthy of responsive (for example, productive adaptive) involvement.

Kojima's model for TD/FDI was that of US firms' investment in other developed countries in the decades following 1945. This FDI occurred, he argues, in industries where there was no immediate loss of comparative advantage in the US, so that continued supply of overseas markets through exports remained possible. Though US enterprises at this time possessed the strong OAs that allowed them to carry out FDI, the LAs relevant to those industries remained strong in the US (as a source of comparative advantage), and there was no efficiency-motivated need to carry out international production. The FDI occurred, therefore, as a result of trade restraints or as part of the competitive process in these more concentrated and oligopolistic industries. It can then be interpreted as a defensive response to some other source of threat rather than to any decline in efficiency, which might well be diminished in the process. By associating this 'US-type' of FDI closely with new industries and innovation Kojima (1978, 90) draws attention to its similarities with the behaviour of the second stage of Vernon's PLCM, where exports are replaced by overseas production for reasons that are seen as more likely to be defensive than cost-optimising. He thus adopts (Kojima, 1973, 6) Vernon's list of product cycle industries (the highly innovative and strongly oligopolistic chemical, machinery, transportation equipment and scientific instrument sectors) as exemplifying the sources of US TD/FDI.[5]

Overall, we see a central aim of Kojima's theorising as being to place FDI within a dynamic theory of the international division of labour, and from this to derive meaningful conclusions regarding productive efficiency and economic growth. In co-opting this towards the analysis of IB we place the spotlight on its elucidation of the nature of location advantages and their implications for strategic choices made by MNEs. In the case of TC/FDI we interpret the presence of positive LAs reflecting a host-country's comparative advantage (input costs and efficiencies) as determining aggressive ES-location choices by MNEs that see these as enhancing profitability levels above those previously available. By contrast the TD/FDI case represents defensive strategic behaviour in which the MNE responds to negative LAs (notably restraints on trade) through MS investments in order to protect as much as possible of the profitability lost in diversion from a preferred supply through trade.

So far this analysis has focused predominantly on the short-term implications of LAs; how they determine the roles played by MNE subsidiaries at a point in time. But there are also important dynamic issues to be resolved. Here it is crucial to recall that *changes* in LAs are endogenous to development; they can be both a challenge to and a source of sustainable growth. We addressed this issue in terms of firm-level dynamics in the discussion of ES behaviour in the network hierarchy. There we noted that whereas changing LAs (higher priced but more efficient inputs) could render an ES operation's initial supply role vulnerable to 'footloose' relocation the subsidiary could upgrade to a higher-value-added more productive status based around similarly upgraded inputs (developmental LAs). Kojima offers a similar interpretation in his presentation of 'orderly' technology transfer and a potential 'tutor' role for inward FDI.

'ORDERLY' AND 'DISORDERLY' TECHNOLOGY TRANSFER

The context for Kojima's orderly development-supporting technology transfer is that of TC/FDI. Because this involves the transfer of the FDI package from a developed country (C1) to a less-developed country (C2) it is plausible to assume that the first industries to lose comparative advantage in C1 will be those based on low-technology standardised production processes that mainly use the unskilled labour that is a presumed positive LA of C2. The technologies embodying those processes are not only the ones most suitable to activating those attributes relevant to the incipient industries in C2, but are also based on skill types that can be most easily taught in a learning-by-doing training process. Then, Kojima indicates, having assimilated these most basic competences C2 can eventually move on to the next level in technological evolution and effectively learn that. Kojima thus asserts that TC/FDI provides the basis for orderly technology transfer and underpins a sustainable process that is based around the logical evolution of the host-country comparative advantage.

In his detailed exposition of these potentials Kojima places emphasis on Joint Ventures as the most viable institution for securing the desired transmission and assimilation of knowledge, skills and technologies (OAs). Such an alliance between foreign investors and local enterprise would involve both parties in 'the common pursuit of profits' so that they would 'be sharing responsibilities and solving technical and managerial problems as they arise' (Kojima, 1978).[6] If the process is activated through an appropriate industry, achieving the efficiency optimising complementarity of OAs and LAs presented by TC/FDI, then completion of the localisation process will not only have secured fully competitive production but also have allowed all the relevant competences to have been learnt by local personnel. This parallels the articulation of appropriate technology transfer that had emerged by that time in IB analysis. But a valuable addition of Kojima's exposition is then to project the basis for an endogenous repetition and prolongation of the process.

Once an industry at the lower end of the technology ladder has been effectively established and indigenised Kojima's approach asserts that the preconditions will have been fulfilled for the potential to now exist to allow the repeat of a similar sequence of events so as to localise another industry of a somewhat higher degree of technical ambition. The reasoning behind the assumed feasibility of this next step is that the technology acquired and assimilated in operationalising the first industry would not only have had an industry-specific component (the foreign firm's OAs), but also a wider contextual influence. It would, hopefully, have introduced and effectively transmitted an understanding of new industrial practices and organisational routines, so that the platform for more advanced learning will have been inculcated. Schematically, the industrial base in C2 will become ready to access (as TC/FDI) the new least comparatively advantaged industry in C1. There can be a repeat of the 'foreign firm as tutor' process to initiate and embed this next industry. Thus Kojima envisages an orderly sequence of foreign investments that will support the systematic enrichment of a host-country's industrial environment. This will then provide for a steady development process that is able to access and benefit from appropriate technology transfers. These can start from relatively simple labour-intensive sectors and processes and evolve gradually towards those that are more capital intensive and that implement relatively sophisticated operations.

To characterise the contrary possibility of *dis*orderly (or inappropriate) technology transfer we can construct a hybrid case where FDI flows from a comparatively advantaged industry in a developed economy (such as C3 in the TD/FDI scenario) but into a developing economy where (unlike C2 in TC/FDI) there is no potential comparative advantage for this industry. This, in fact, more or less exemplifies the import-substitution industrial strategy that we saw adopted in some Latin American countries in the 1950s and provides an explanation for its revealed inefficiency and inability to generate the foundations for sustainable industrial development. Two factors underline this. Firstly, the FDI is not undertaken because of any perceived complementarity with local input conditions. The LAs that attract these industries are (in a TD/FDI manner) a reasonably significant local market (that probably only exists in such an economy as a result of a highly skewed income distribution) to which MNEs have become denied access through protectionist barriers (negative LAs generating MS subsidiaries). Secondly, the technology transferred (the OAs to be activated) is likely to be sophisticated and both capital and skill intensive, reflecting its origins in successful consumer-oriented industries in an advanced economy. The 'infant industry' propagated has no plausible scope to reach the country's true sources of comparative advantage. The technology gap between the FDI industry and that reflecting the country's potential is, in effect, maximised; rather than minimised in the TC/FDI case. This precludes any extensive or appropriate learning of technological, managerial or marketing skills by indigenous personnel. It also suggests that where the MNE's competencies are learnt locally their relatively sophisticated nature (and high rewards) will make the recipients members of an elite industrial enclave that is more closely associated with foreign-dominated sectors than with the wider economy. It exacerbates development constraining dualism and an urban-rural imbalance.

NOTES

1. Kojima (1973, 4) lists these industries as 'such traditional industries as textiles, clothing and processing of steel' and more modern labour-intensive operations in the form of 'assembly of motor vehicles, production of parts and components of radios and other electronic machines'.
2. In another important pioneering attempt to understand the nature and timing of Japanese FDI Ozawa (1979a, 1979b) generalises the outward-push factors as an escape from the 'Ricardo-Hicks trap of industrialisation. Thus the success of Japan's post-war industrial growth led to the *need* to escape from growing constraints (rising wage rates, scarcities of land, energy and raw materials) and the malignancies of pollution, congestion and ecological destruction' (Ozawa, 1979b, 84–9) and the *ability* to do so by leveraging the availability of capital, foreign exchange, competitive firm-level competences and access to established international markets.
3. Ozawa (1991) later documented the manner in which distinctive stages in the growth and spread of Japan's overseas investments were closely interdependent with the path of industrial restructuring in the home-country economy.
4. The consequences of such TD/FDI to C4 on the rest of the C3 industry's trade is contingent, notably on whether C4's creation of trade barriers is part of a more widespread move towards protectionism so that its implications are replicated elsewhere. If we assume that this does not happen and the trade option otherwise remains open then the effect depends on whether the loss of C3 output affects the industry's efficiency. This could have negative effects on productivity through loss of economies of scale.
5. Kojima (1982, 15) elaborated the ways in which US FDI in such sectors not only lowered welfare in a general sense but also contributed directly to specific problems in the domestic economy. Thus, he argues, 'it should also be remembered that it was hasty American direct investment abroad on the part of her most sophisticated industries, those ranked at the top of her comparative advantage structure, which brought about her present difficulties, such as the loss of international competitiveness, deterioration in balance of

trade, unemployment, and inflation'. It was not a plausible part of a positive structural adjustment process.

6. Kojima extended this to adopt the concept (fashionable in the 1970s as part of the FDI component in the debate on a New International Economic Order) of a 'fade out' Joint Venture (Hirschman, 1969). Thus Kojima (1978, 94–5) suggests 'a progressive transfer of ownership may be necessary if the genuine objective of foreign direct investment is not a permanent source of monopoly profits but the complementation of deficient factors in the recipient country'.

6. Internalisation: ownership advantage as an intermediate good

In earlier chapters we have introduced two of the key tenets of IB analysis. To become an MNE a firm needs a unique source of competitive advantage and a reason to apply this within value-adding activities in an overseas location. The analysis so far then implies a further assumption; the competitive advantage is *transferred* to the foreign location in a hierarchically organised process between parts of the firm. This assumption remained to be analytically validated. Internalised transfer was a choice made amongst alternatives. This questioning of the internal transfer assumption had both analytical and practical perspectives. Analytically, the recognition of firm-specific competitive advantages (OAs) as intermediate *goods* opened the potential for their externalisation through a market transaction. If a plausible local firm exists in the relevant foreign economy why not sell the OA to it, avoiding the risks and costs of FDI? Early IB theorising already provided a provenance for such speculation, since the potential local firm would be fully embedded in the institutions of the relevant economy and the costs of 'liability of foreignness' would be avoided. At the level of practicalities market arrangements for such sources of competitiveness were clearly emerging by the early 1970s: licensing (for technologies), management contracts (for such practices and procedures), trademark licensing (for reputation) and franchising (for service industry routines). Where a firm became an MNE and expanded through acts of FDI it was rejecting such market options. Internalisation theory as introduced by Buckley and Casson (1976) set out to explain why.

It is important to immediately be clear that the 'home' territory of internalisation is the theory of the firm; it does not, in and of itself, involve any prioritised referencing of international transactions. Thus a predominant concern of the classic texts (Coase, 1937; Williamson, 1975, 1979, 1985) that underpin the key precepts of internalisation thinking (in terms of market failures for intermediate goods) was the boundaries of the firm. Which value-adding activities were better controlled hierarchically within the organisational structures of the firm itself and which intermediate goods could be reliably accessed externally through arm's-length (or contractual) market arrangements with independent enterprises? It is only

when LAs determine that one party to a potential intermediate good transaction is located overseas that internalisation analysis becomes relevant to
the decision as to whether or not the firm needs to operate as an MNE to
secure the available potential. Of course, as was often argued, contracting
for market-based transactions for intermediate goods between independent firms was often likely to be more difficult if the two parties were in
different locations and from different institutional backgrounds. But this
was not intrinsic to the dominant modes of thinking on internalisation
derived from the theory of the firm. Besides, by the same token, organising an internal hierarchical transfer between two parts of the same firm
in such different locations was also likely to be more fraught and costly
than between units in the same institutional and cultural jurisdiction. The
defining comparison central to the contribution of internalisation here is
still that between two modes of organising a particular intermediate good
transaction, the major determinant is then the nature of the good to be
transferred and the degree of difficulty likely to be involved in contracting
for a market-based transaction for it.

From this we can see that as a concept in IB internalisation operates
at two levels: as an overarching theoretical *principle* and as an organising
management *practice*. As a broad-brush principle we have seen that to be
an MNE a firm needs to be internalising cross-border intermediate goods
transactions. But an important function of such abstract theorising is to
facilitate the understanding of the behaviour of real-world cases. To fully
address the organisational practice of a particular MNE would require the
application of relevant aspects of the theory of the firm (uncertainties;
transaction costs; opportunism; asymmetric information; small number
conditions; bargaining costs; switching costs) to each of the many intermediate good transactions it chooses to internalise due to imperfections
in possible external (arm's-length or contractual) markets for them. There
are, of course, an incalculable number of intermediate goods involved in
the operations of MNEs and the global economy more widely. For this
reason meaningful elucidation of internalisation as an organisational
practice has tended to proceed through analysis of precise cases, of specific intermediates, firms or industries. However, as indicated by Buckley
(1990), the most influential contexts for internalisation decisions within an
MNE may be closely related to that firm's wider organisational structure
and dominant strategic imperatives. In line with that we can here suggest a
provisional tripartite typology of internalisation decisions related to their
firm's prevalent competitive nature.

Firstly, we can assert the central importance of 'outward' internalisation. Here the relevant intermediate goods are the (mainly intangible)
sources of owned and controlled (in early theorising also centrally created)

competitive advantages (OAs) which define the firm's ability to expand internationally and which become central to the implementation of overseas value-adding activities. The analytical importance of this type of internalisation was implicit in the emergence of MNEs as multi-domestic or network hierarchies as described in Chapter 4. We can also see this as the most 'strategic' of the types of internalisation, since not only do the transferred attributes represent the current competitive bases of the firm but also serve to determine the precise strategic role expected of the recipient overseas operation and assert the nature of its position in the wider organisation of the MNE.

Next we can invoke 'inward' internalisation decisions. Here the intermediates are 'secondary' inputs (component parts; raw materials; support services) to a value-added process that is developed around the implementation of the roles and needs that are defined by the 'primary' inputs (OAs). Beyond strict IB this has been traditionally discussed as a 'make or buy' decision, or with an international component as 'offshoring'. When the preferred source of such an input is in a different economy from that of the intended user, and the firm decides to secure reliable access through the ownership and control of the supplier, the resulting international intermediate goods transfer becomes an 'inward' internalisation process organised to benefit the performance of an MNE.[1] We can consider these inward internalisation decisions and the associated transactions as 'tactical' by comparison with the strategic implications of the 'outward' version. Thus the sourcing decisions implemented through inward internalisation are based on the need to fulfil in the most effective way possible input requirements that are defined by the role allocated to the facility and determined by the primary/strategic attributes of the MNE. This type of intra-group sourcing will become much more prevalent in NH than they would have been in the MH. Though the ES subsidiaries in the NH are located where they are precisely because that location can provide key inputs in a highly effective way, the open networked mindset increasingly endemic to these organisations would also generate a willingness to source other inputs (less readily available in the selected location) from other facilities in the group. The global supply network of the NH is not by any means constrained to final product subsidiaries.[2]

Thirdly, we can suggest 'vertical' internalisation, which operates within firms formulated as vertically integrated MNEs. The vertically integrated MNE operates through a sequence of value-adding processes, of which several will be in different countries. These take a particular commodity from usually raw material exploitation through various refining and semi-manufacturing stages into various marketed final products. The intermediate goods that link these sequential processes within the vertically integrated MNE are thus subject to vertical internalisation. In a fully configured vertically integrated MNE each subsidiary would receive an intermediate good from another part of the firm, add value to it in a process its host economy is suited to supporting and then transfer it onwards, as an upgraded intermediate, to the next stage in the sequence in a different location.

Conceptualising *vertical internalisation* then contributes to this formulation by explaining why such international intermediate-goods transactions are also intra-firm transfers, linking two different value-adding processes under common ownership and control. We can enter three speculations regarding the application of internalisation arguments to an analysis of when and where vertically integrated MNEs might emerge. Firstly, the whole sequence of stages is based on the competitive evolution of a very specific initiating commodity that will remain at its core. This may mean that causes of market failure for that commodity as the first (internalised) intermediate may continue to pervade its later manifestations as upgraded intermediates and also mandate their internalised transfer. But, secondly, the later transfers will be between different host countries, with different institutional environments and accessible types of organisational skills. This may make it more feasible to operate through arm's-length markets or contractual arrangements at these later stages. Internalisation benefits as a reason for continued vertical integration may weaken and the sequence break down. Thirdly, a great strength of an experienced vertically integrated MNE may be in competences in organising and coordinating such international intra-firm transfers (a type of OA). Ultimately, the MNE as a group benefits from overseeing the whole sequence, even if some of the separate intermediate goods transfers might have been at least as effectively implemented through external transaction modes.

TECHNOLOGY TRANSFERS – 'BUYER' AND 'SELLER' UNCERTAINTY

In their pioneering exposition and positioning of internalisation in theorising the MNE Buckley and Casson (1976, 39–40, 45) place major emphasis on the problems of organising external markets for the knowledge and intangible assets that underpin those firms' competitiveness and potential for expansion. We follow that precedent here by focusing on technology (and by implication other intangible sources of firm-level competitiveness) as exemplifying the types of market failures central to internalisation. Here technology, we will suggest, encompasses both the theoretical and practical faces of our analytical perspectives. Not only does technology as an intermediate good, decisively possess characteristics that severely test the viability of external markets but it also sits, as earlier chapters have demonstrated, at the core of the competitive advantages likely to drive the internationalisation of many potential MNEs. Indeed in terms we have just introduced, technology would be the most plausible candidate for 'outward' internalisation in the emergence and activation of the hierarchically structured MNEs.[3]

We can immediately observe the paradox that renders technology the definitive candidate for the types of market failure that led to internalisation. Any market will work more efficiently the more easily and completely information about the goods to be transacted can be disseminated amongst the participants. The need would be to remove any trace of buyer or seller uncertainty, so that a price can be agreed at the core of a transaction-cost-free trade. But where the good to be transacted is some form of intangible knowledge (such as technology) then uncertainty-removing information about its precise details and characteristics *cannot* be freely communicated; it would 'give away' the good itself. The inevitable persistence of both buyer and seller uncertainty would vastly complicate any moves towards an agreement in a potential market for technology. Such a market would be, at best, massively imperfect and inefficient, involving potentially prohibitive transaction costs.

We can start with the familiar problem of buyer uncertainty. In perfect competition, of course, it is assumed that buyers are fully informed (probably from past experience of the good) of the characteristics of their intended purchase and so have no questions over their decisions. But if the possible purchase is technology that they are considering the transaction is possible precisely because they *don't* know its details but believe it *might* fill a gap in their competences in a valuable way. However, the details of the technology cannot be passed to them in advance of the transaction. Means by which buyer uncertainty could be vitiated in the case of some goods are not viable here. In the case of commodity of presumed homogeneous, but initially unknown, quality (such as a grain crop) a *sample* could be provided. Full analysis of this is available to the potential buyer and can then facilitate an informed offer. This is not feasible for technology. One facet of an intrinsically heterogeneous body of technology could not serve as a plausible indicator of the ability of the whole to fit with the perceived needs of the potential purchaser.

Another mechanism for overcoming buyer uncertainty would be to offer a trial of the good (household consumer durables, perhaps, or a trial run of a vehicle) with the option of return if not satisfactory. For technology this would mean access to the complete body of knowledge, to be assessed in terms of its practical value in conjunction with the potential recipient's extant capabilities. But here *return* of a rejected technology would mean *forgetting* it after full involvement with its characteristics and potentials. Even setting aside the obvious scope for opportunism, this is not realistic. Once a firm's top scientists, technologists and engineers have been sufficiently involved with the technology and to have fully understood it they cannot, in the very nature of their professional mindset, forget it. Even if they genuinely saw no immediate potential in it, it will have become an unavoidable part of the knowledge base from which their future exploratory considerations will derive. We will see this line of argument recurring as a part of seller uncertainty.

For the moment we can see that the issue of asymmetrical information underlying buyer uncertainty cannot be fully removed from the possible market for technology. Nevertheless, a potential purchaser of a particular body of technology might feel a sufficient degree of intuitive expectation that it *could* turn out to fill a perceived gap in its own scope to be willing to enter into a bargaining process over it. But it will still do this with considerable persisting doubts over whether the technology would indeed generate the degree of improvement in its future income stream that it would have expected from an ideal source. It will therefore build a significant risk discount into its bargaining stance. So the upper limit of its offer range in the bargaining would be kept low, at least by comparison to the offer it would have been prepared to make for a technology about which it was fully informed and confident of its ability to generate the intended improved income stream. The buyer's maximum offer will be kept low.

Though 'seller uncertainty' is not as widespread in practice, or an analytical concern, as 'buyer uncertainty' we can argue strongly here that the market for technology is one context where it possesses very considerable relevance. Sellers of most mass-market consumer goods and, indeed, of many intermediate goods have no reason to be concerned about how the purchasers will use the product. Its use is usually predetermined and constrained to functions that will have no implications for the current or future performance of the seller. This, we will argue, is categorically not the case for the technologies and other intangible attributes that comprise OAs, of MNEs.

Once again asymmetrical information is an important aspect of the issue. This time the constraint is on how much the selling firm can know about the potential purchasing firm and its specific abilities and intentions for the use of the technology. There will be a considerable reservation in the possible buyer's willingness to explain exactly why it needs the technology.[4] There is also an 'appropriability' issue here. The seller would wish to be confident that the terms of the transaction allow it to appropriate its share of the revenue and other benefits the buyer obtains from the technology. Not knowing this a priori may be one reason why the seller sets a high price in entering the bargaining process; it wishes to cover the risk of 'giving away' an asset that proves to be of unforeseen value to the purchaser. But a more important uncertainty for the seller will be the extent to which the successful use of the technology by the buyer turns out to be at the expense of its own competitive operations.

To elaborate this we need to observe that a firm's current technology and other intangible competitive competences have two distinct uses. The first is its current embodiment in the firm's successful established products and production processes. Secondly, the technology's evolutionary potentials as a basis for ongoing research agendas and future innovations. The sale of such technology to another enterprise may then constitute some degree of threat to both these values. The extent of this threat will depend on the current capacities and exploratory potentials of the buyer, which as we have emphasised, are likely to be disguised from the seller as much as possible.

The central threat that is likely to come under consideration by a firm licensing its technology to an independent enterprise in another country is that when that licensee uses the technology to produce goods that are the same or in close rivalry to its own (as is logically very likely) this can eat into the revenue stream that it expects to earn from those capabilities. The established response has been to build geographical market restrictions into the licensing contract. The licensee agrees to sell its output only into markets agreed with the licensor; probably only its own domestic market and selected (perhaps regionally contiguous) markets that the licensor is prepared to opt out of. Building such terms into a contract and ensuring their enactment will, however, involve very significant *transaction costs*. High-quality personnel will be committed to an often contentious, fraught and prolonged bargaining process; expensive legal expertise is then needed to formulate the agreement; resources committed to monitoring compliance and, if necessary, more legal expenses required if deviance from the contracted terms needs to be addressed.

The longer-term threat is that the rival firm may indeed progress the licensed technology in a more original and innovative way. If this happens the licensor could, in a few years' time, find itself facing new products introduced by its licensee that include much more inventive and competitive evolutions of its own original knowledge sources. How plausible this threat is, at the point of contracting, may be difficult for a licensor to predict, again due to lack of detailed knowledge of the licensee. Again it adds to seller uncertainty. Though clauses in licensing agreements have been devised to attempt to mitigate this threat,[5] they are likely to be even more complex in negotiation, stipulation in legally rigorous terms, monitoring and legal enforcement. The transactions costs are again formidable.

This focus on seller uncertainty provides us with two, analytically interrelated, reasons why the market for technology may be prone to failure, with the result that firms possessing strong knowledge-based sources of competitiveness may internalise them and, where relevant circumstances determine, opt to expand internationally. Firstly, and more simply, experience of the endemically high transactions costs of even attempting to deal with the uncertainties of licensing may eventually lead to an unequivocal policy of not even considering selling technology. Where the firms have such competitive advantages that need overseas use they automatically become MNEs. Secondly, the firm may persist in considering possible licensing opportunities. But, for reasons reviewed earlier, they would accept a need to discount, to some degree, their own future income stream due to uncontrolled threats from the licensor's output. To offset this they would need to set a high price (royalty) for the technology and create an adequate alternative income stream. The seller's minimum offer price will be kept high. Ultimately, upward pressure on the price acceptable to sellers (reflecting seller uncertainty) and the downward pressure as the price offered by potential buyers (due to their uncertainty) may result in no overlap in acceptable prices existing. Negotiation would reveal that the market had failed. No deal could be made and the owner of the technology will retain its internalised use.

INTERNALISATION AND ECONOMIC PERFORMANCE

Logically enough, most of the discussion of internalisation has itself been 'internalised' to contexts constrained to the MNE; how it is organised and how it aims to optimise the returns it gets from operationalisation of its unique sources of competitive advantage as intermediate goods. But its implications can be seen to have a wider context if we seek to address the qualitative or normative context of MNE behaviour and performance. The basis for the internalisation decision, as we have been reviewing it here, is that an opportunity exists in a particular economy whose competitive viability is predicated on the efficient application of a firm-level advantage initially owned by a foreign firm (an MNE's OAs) to sources of competitiveness innate to that location (LAs). The normative economic question that we can then raise is whether the potentials of the project, from the point of view of the *host-country's* needs, will be best realised if the firm-specific attributes needed are acquired (licensed) by a local firm (externalised) or are retained and implemented by the foreign firm (internalisation by an MNE).

Even if we assume that the performance aspirations for the project remain the same irrespective of whether it is implemented by an MNE subsidiary or an independent local firm it is plausible that the degree of achievement may differ.[6] This could occur due to different abilities in achieving the common objective of securing the perceived potentials from combining the OAs with the relevant LAs. Differences in such suboptimal performance, we suggest, might reflect different capacities to understand, adapt to and assimilate the 'alien' component of the combination. A local firm licensing the OA will, hopefully, fully understand the local inputs it will access and/or the local market it will target (the LAs). But it will be initially unfamiliar with the OAs, precisely because, as the theory has pointed out, it cannot be fully appraised of their details a priori. The time taken to learn and accurately operationalise these OAs will, at least temporarily, compromise efficiency. But whilst the MNE subsidiary would be expected to very quickly understand the internalised OAs it will need time to overcome the general liabilities of foreignness and to fully comprehend the details of the opportunity to be addressed. It will need to understand the full characteristics and potentials of the LAs. The differing capacities to mitigate the relevant unfamiliarities might well lead to differing levels of performance resulting from the internalisation/externalisation choice.

NOTES

1. It is worth noting that such a supplier, even when internalised by an MNE, may not *only* supply other parts of the parent group. Where it does not compromise competitiveness of other units of the MNE it may still supply, through more open-market transactions, independent customers.
2. A major illustration here, of course, would be an ES subsidiary that is primarily an assembly operation, leveraging cheap labour as the defining host-country LA. Components to be assembled may be sourced from other (also ES) subsidiaries in other countries.
3. Buckley and Casson (1976, 45) thus state categorically that 'internalisation of the knowledge market will generate a high degree of multinationality among firms'. This will come about because 'knowledge is a public good which is easily transmitted across national boundaries [so that] its exploitation is logically an international operation'. Unless particular conditions such as comparative advantage 'restrict production to a single country, internalisation of knowledge will require each firm to operate a network of plants on a world-wide basis'.
4. To elucidate this in detail would involve the buyer outlining details of its own extant technologies and precisely how it would expect these to be strengthened by the newly acquired technologies. For reasons of its own competitiveness it will obviously be very constrained in revealing such information.
5. These include prohibitions on any form of adjustment to the licensed technology, or exclusion of any form of R&D based on it. Alternatively, the 'grant back' arrangements

stipulated that any knowledge or product development secured by the licensee that was based on or incorporated licensed technology would have to be freely 'granted back' to the licensor. This would be expected to sufficiently limit the competitive advantage available to the licensee from such exploration that it becomes competitively unviable.

6. We exclude, for example, any difference in the defined objective of a local firm under the influence of perceived country-level development objectives.

7. The knowledge-seeking transition: decentralising innovation and R&D

INTRODUCTION

The most pervasive assumption so far in this narrative has been that MNEs emerged and expanded on the basis of centrally derived sources of competitive advantage that reflected their home-country knowledge base. But, as we noted at the end of Chapter 3, once such firms had matured as internationally oriented entities this positioning would begin to change. As they themselves mature, subsidiaries, especially those in more developed economies and with an MS orientation, are likely to become more assertive and seek to individualise their own competitive competences. They are likely to do this by internalising knowledge sources from their host economies. Where such subsidiaries succeed in doing this, we will argue, they can play creative roles within the competitive dynamics of both their host country and their parent MNE group. Ultimately these 'creative subsidiaries' (Pearce, 1999) activate such a distinctive and individualising positioning through an ability to operate effectively within two knowledge-based communities, that of their MNE group and that of their host economy. Once MNEs learnt to understand and embrace such subsidiary-level initiative and competence creation (Cantwell and Mudambi, 2005) their overall organisational structures become reconfigured as heterarchies (Hedlund, 1986, 1993; Birkinshaw, 1994) or transnationals (Bartlett and Ghoshal, 1989, 1990).

We can place these strategic developments within our broader picture as being the MNEs' response to a third significant change in the global economy. The first two of these changes, we saw in Chapter 4, were the lowering of restraints on trade and the emergence of a significant number of new MNEs. The immediate result of this was to greatly enhance the competitiveness of the international markets for firms' mature and established goods and to provoke the MNEs' move towards a network of cost-effective ES subsidiaries aiming to secure price-competitive supply of this current product range. This, therefore, specifically targeted what we distinguish as their first overarching strategic aim; to maximise the performance secured from their existing, already effectively operationalised, sources of competitiveness. The third change in the global economy, we will argue here, then provoked a similarly enhanced emphasis on the second defining competitive priority, to upgrade these core sources of competitiveness as quickly, responsively and thoroughly as possible. Here we refer to the increasing emergence of more countries (and often specific locations, such as knowledge clusters, within countries) that possessed strong and distinctively original sources of *creative* inputs into such firm-level pursuit of competitive enhancement.

To trace how these new knowledge sources emerged within the developmental processes of increasing numbers of countries we can adopt a distinction (Pearce and Zhang, 2010; Zhang and Pearce, 2012, 33–40) between 'level-2' and 'level-3' resources. Here we perceive level-2 resources as 'standardised inputs into mature and successful production processes ... [which] can be upgraded *within* the development process'[1] (Pearce and Zhang, 2010, 484). As the most pervasively influential of such level-2 resources the labour supply can be upgraded to higher productivity levels, through both improved education of new entrants to the labour force and systematic support for retraining of incumbents. Similarly, the energy supply can be improved through time, in terms of both its price and reliability. Again the ability of key elements of infrastructure, such as transport systems, ports, airports and communications and IT, can be systematically enhanced so as to support industrial growth. In the terms already adopted here level-2 resources are likely to serve as positive LAs, attracting mainly ES operations of MNEs, though they would also be supportive of effectiveness in MS supply of the local market. Crucially, it is the facility to upgrade level-2 resources that, as we have argued, can embed ES subsidiaries into sustainable industrialisation and refute the 'footloose' danger.

However, a second defining feature of level-2 resources is that though their upgrading allows them to play higher-value-added roles they do not themselves possess the capacity to affect this role. They cannot influence the technologies they work with or the production processes to which they will be inputs. Thus 'upgrading level-2 resources is *necessary* for persisting growth, but it will not be *sufficient*. The chance to apply them will depend on the availability of new opportunities opened up by access to new technologies and to sources of technological progress' (Pearce and Zhang, 2010, 485). The ability of inward investments by MNEs to play this role has already been described here, notably for example, in Kojima's scenario of trade-creating FDI and its dynamic manifestation in the potential for orderly technology transfer. However, it would be clearly a logical aim of a truly *national* economic development process to escape from such technological dependency. It would require support for the local generation of the new opportunities for the competitive utilisation of the upgraded level-2 resources. Addressing this issue in the sustainability of national development leads countries to support the generation of level-3 resources, which will have 'the capacity to contribute to the *local* derivation of new knowledge-driven developmental potentials'. They 'will have no association with current supply of standardised goods' but provide 'the resources that help define *new* directions and opportunities for development' (Pearce and Zhang, 2010, 490).

The practicalities of generating level-3 resources within an economy were reflected in the increasing adoption of national systems of innovation (NSI), which can be seen as 'complex and ever evolving nexus of creative inputs and learning processes mediated by associated institutions . . . [such as] the education system, research laboratories (private, public and university), enterprise and government supports' (Pearce and Zhang, 2010, 490). The level-3 resources that manifest the ability of an NSI to interject creative dynamism into an economy should then be 'technology, skills, inventiveness and imagination' embodied in 'individuals, teams, firms, knowledge-support infrastructure and technology policies' (Pearce and Zhang, 2010, 490). Success for such policies would be seen in terms of the ability of the economy to export goods based on their originality and distinctive quality, rather than simply the capacity to produce them at a lower cost than alternative locations. These dimensions of competitive originality then derive from individualising attributes in the underlying level-3 resources, in terms of very distinctive new areas of scientific and technological leadership and a range of creative elements of human capital (market researchers, inventive engineers, entrepreneurial risk-oriented managers). But whilst growth of these level-3 attributes is likely to be benefitting from path-dependency and the forces of agglomeration within the development of the domestic economy they remain open to co-option and internalisation in the innovation processes of any firms that recognise a distinctive and relevant creative potential in them; including MNEs. From this perspective such attributes become sources of created dynamic comparative advantage, which may be seen as a new form of LA by MNEs and possibly be appropriated by them in their own globalised KS ambitions.

We thus return to a dynamic interface between MNEs' need to regenerate their OAs through R&D and innovation and the pursuit of knowledge-based sources of competitiveness by individual economies. Viewed within the perspectives of such an interactive evolution we discuss three interrelated facets of this. Firstly, the emergence of decentralised approaches to innovation as activated through subsidiaries that begin to acquire strategic capacities and influences. Secondly, the decentralisation of R&D operations in ways that can play different roles in the knowledge-based pursuit of new dimensions of competitiveness. Thirdly, how these decentralising and geographically diversifying processes changed the organisational structures and challenges of MNEs in becoming, for example, heterarchies or transnationals. Endemic to all these, in terms of MNEs' strategic diversity, is the motivation of knowledge seeking. This can be defined as 'the pursuit by MNEs of new technological capabilities, scientific capacity (research facilities) and creative expertise (e.g. dimensions of tacit knowledge) from *particular* host countries, in order to extend the *overall* competences (product range and core technology) of the group' (Manea and Pearce, 2004, 4).[2]

DECENTRALISATION OF INNOVATION AND THE EXTENSION OF SUBSIDIARY ROLES

The roots of the initial perception of an emerging presence of decentralisation of innovation in MNEs can be found, mainly in Canada in the early 1980s, in the discovery of subsidiaries that were undertaking that responsibility. Indeed, we can contend that this discovery of *innovation* by subsidiaries also represented the discovery of the *subsidiary* itself as a specific and important level of analytical discussion in IB. Up to this point the dominance of hierarchical perceptions of MNE organisational structure meant that, as a consequence of the centralised generation of the firms' sources of international competitiveness, subsidiaries would be entirely dependent and submissive. The role they played (MS or ES) would be determined for them by the home-country parent HQ, which would also be the source of their ability to play it. Reflecting this our discussion here will interrelate two important new themes in discussion of the MNE. Firstly, the analysis of the specific types of subsidiaries that performed such innovation activities as part of the competitive evolution of their MNE group. Secondly, how this particular role became understood as one amongst a range of differently motivated and structured roles that subsidiaries could play. Thus the pioneering delineation of typologies for the roles of subsidiaries indicated, more precisely than before, the strategic diversity of MNEs, thereby pointing towards the soon-to-emerge understanding of MNEs as heterarchies or transnationals.

The foundations of this new phase in analysis of MNEs can be seen in the discovery of the 'product mandate' subsidiary in Canada (Rugman, 1983; Poynter and Rugman, 1982). The distinctive break from traditional expectations of subsidiary positioning that was discerned in these pioneering case studies was that operations of, mainly US, MNEs in Canada were not only producing but also developing goods for the whole North American market and perhaps beyond. As indicated by the adoption of the term 'mandate' it was understood that this new subsidiary-level responsibility and power was recognised, authorised and supported by HQ. Another vital point recognised in the Canadian debate over such roles was that securing such developmental roles in foreign-owned operations should also reflect, build on and help enhance, dynamic qualities of the host economy. In IB terms a new type of creative LA emerges. From these intuitive initial insights the concept was gradually embedded in the wider perceptions of the MNE, so that a later definition (Papanastassiou and Pearce, 1999, 28) saw the PM as a subsidiary that received a mandate from the parent company 'to take responsibility for the creation of particular products, and for their sustained competitive evolution, as well as their production and marketing'.

An important spin-off from the challenge to the accepted unambitious expectations for subsidiary roles that was provoked by the discovery of PMs was the pioneering typology of such roles derived by White and Poynter (1984). We can term this as a 'scope typology', since the three dimensions with the potential to discriminate between such subsidiaries would represent facets of their scope, in terms of competitive positioning and in-house capabilities. The first of these is *product* scope, defined as 'the latitude exercised by a subsidiary's business with regard to product line extensions and new product areas'. Taken with the options defined within their typology itself we find White and Poynter implying both static and dynamic dimensions of the possible product scope of a subsidiary. Firstly, it can reflect persistence of technological dependency in the subsidiary by posing the question as to how much of the parent group's existing product range the subsidiary will produce. This provides a clear dichotomy between MS- and ES-oriented subsidiaries. Here an MS subsidiary is likely to have an extensive product range, covering all the group's mature goods for which the host-economy *demand* structure generates an adequate (protected) market. Then an ES subsidiary would focus on a much narrower product scope, comprising those where local input (*supply*-side) conditions determine a basis for cost-competitive production. The second factor in product scope is whether the subsidiary possesses the capacity and permission to *develop* new products that become unique to its own competences, or remains constrained to supply of the group's mature range; that is, whether it can aspire to KS responsibilities and an innovation role.

The second dimension in the typology is then *market* scope, in terms of 'the range of geographic markets available to the subsidiary'. Though the precise range of external markets the subsidiary might supply (regional or fully global) can carry significant organisational and strategic implications, market scope is most basically perceived as a host-market/export-market dichotomy. The former is then the province of an MS subsidiary and the latter that of the ES. Though less definitionally clear-cut we would then expect an effective KS subsidiary to have quite an extensive market scope. The degree of originality implied in a successful product development outcome would be likely to secure significant international markets, and a realistic expectation of such an extensive market would probably have been built into a subsidiary's case for securing such high-cost creative responsibilities.

Finally, *value-added (or functional)* scope 'refers to the range of ways a subsidiary adds value, whether through development, manufacturing or marketing activities'. This, therefore, asks how many of the core functions that would be essential to the competitive *development* and *operation* of a fully defined enterprise are activated within a particular subsidiary. The important distinction for the analysis here becomes that between the dependent MS/ES roles, that encompass the quite constrained elements of routine functional scope that are needed to secure effective hierarchically imposed performance and the more speculative dynamics of the KS roles that can draw in exploratory and creative functions, such as various aspects of R&D work, ambitious market research, inventive engineering and entrepreneurial risk-embracing subsidiary-level management.

In their own path-breaking version of the scope typology White and Poynter (1984, 60) allocate the MS role to a *miniature replica*, subsidiary, which 'produces and markets some of the parent's product lines in the local country [so that] generally the business is a small scale replica of the parent'.[3] They then build on this broad characterisation by distinguishing three variants of the MS role and, in doing so, point towards two emerging phenomena in IB that remain of central concern to us here. Firstly, they indicate the potential for role evolution in subsidiaries and, secondly, demonstrate how this can reflect deepening involvement with the dynamics of the host economy. Here the *adopter* variant takes 'products and marketing programmes from the multinational parent' and applies them with no systematic variation, so that the MNE is depending on a thorough understanding of its mature competitive capacities to establish a bridgehead in a new market environment. Then the *adapter* does 'change product characteristics and marketing to suit local conditions'. This reflects the generalised perception within MNEs of the value of local responsiveness per se and the fact that it becomes viable once a subsidiary has been able to establish secure roots in an economy. Lastly, the *innovator* miniature replica takes the local learning process (as a significant commitment to KS) a stage further by developing new products but in ways that remain closely related to the qualitative bases of the group's existing product range. White and Poynter imply that here innovation is based on mature group technologies as embodied in their mature products, but with scope for the involvement of localised technology sources to generate a significant differentiating strand in product evolution. One surmise that could be read from this progression is that a subsidiary-level impetus towards KS and innovation is most plausible from initial roots in a locally embedded MS subsidiary. Thus these MS roles normally involve a wide product scope, narrow market scope and a functional scope that may start as being quite constrained but widen and take on more adventurous responsibilities as the subsidiary moves towards the innovator variant. An MS subsidiary can deepen its competitive roots in the economy in a logical progression from the adopter to the adapter and then the innovator variants.

For White and Poynter (1984, 61) the ES role is played by a *rationalised manufacturer* that produces 'a designated set of component parts or products for a multi-country or global market'. Similarly in his typology D'Cruz (1986, 88) discerns a *globally rationalised* subsidiary that 'is structured to supply a limited portion of the product line for the entire world market' being a 'production facility [that is] world-scale and concentrates on becoming the low cost producer of those parts of the line for which it is responsible'. With the same emphasis Papanastassiou and Pearce (1999, 27–8) allocate the ES role to a *rationalised product subsidiary*. The terminology used in these cases implies the emergence of the ES subsidiaries as a result of the rationalisation of the extensive product scope of an antecedent MS facility down to a focus on a narrow subset of goods that it can supply very efficiently. An alternative origin for ES subsidiaries would be as new plants in low-cost locations that, because of low-income levels, had not attracted previous MS units. This, as we have argued earlier, would be a result of host-country transition from an import-substitution to an export-oriented development strategy. Compared to the MS role we see these ES subsidiaries as having a narrow product scope and a wide market scope and even narrower and more constrained functional responsibilities.

Though the first use of the *product mandate* terminology in a subsidiary typology was by D'Cruz (1986), White and Poynter themselves derive two variants of the KS product development role. Firstly, the *product specialist* which 'develops, produces and markets a limited product line for global markets'. To achieve this status such a subsidiary needs to generate, through its host-country learning capacities, a degree of self-sufficiency 'in terms of value added by way of applied R&D, production and marketing' (White and Poynter, 1984). But, as with the 'innovator' miniature replica, the product specialist is evolutionary and creates its new competitive competences 'within product areas related to the core business of the multinational parent'. It will not be seeking to challenge the currently dominant technological or business norms of the group.

By contrast White and Poynter find in their *strategic independent* a

KS-oriented subsidiary that does aspire to more radical objectives, through innovations that clearly extend beyond the knowledge base that defines the group's currently dominant scopes. Thus the strategic independents 'have the freedom and resources to develop lines of business for either a local, multi-country or a global market'. For White and Poynter the product specialist accepts the established technologies central to the group's current competitiveness as providing an important guiding input to the innovation process, so that the new good becomes a significant evolutionary step in an orderly competitive progress. But the strategic independent is permitted to place alternative technology sources (presumably mainly host-country accessed) in a much more central role in driving a more revolutionary innovation, with the potential to escape the group's current norms and initiate a new competitive direction.

We can now see the distinction offered intuitively by White and Poynter as pointing towards an important area of analysis in the latter development of debate on subsidiary-level innovation and KS. This analysis sees such innovative and competence-creating subsidiaries as deriving their scope enhancing capacities from a position in two creative knowledge-based communities; that of the parent MNE group and that of the host economy. Then the product specialist privileges the influence of the former technological community and the strategic independent favours the latter.

To finalise the scope typology these KS product mandate type subsidiaries will have a narrow product scope that is focused around products that they have innovated and will be, for a while, the unique supply source. Because of this it will have a wide market scope comprising mandated access to extensive parts of the group's international markets. Its functional/value-added scope will take on creative individualising competences that were definitionally excluded from pure versions of MS or ES.

A key feature of innovation-oriented KS subsidiaries, implicit in the scope typology articulations of their roles, is that they become part of the strategic processes that aim to define the future progress of their group. To reflect this we can review here one more typology of subsidiaries, that of Bartlett and Ghoshal (1986), which focuses on the degree and sources of their strategic status. This generates a four-quadrant categorisation of subsidiaries from two vectors. The first of these is the strategic importance of the subsidiary's host economy, so that the status 'of a specific country unit is strongly influenced by the significance of its national environment to the company's global strategy'. The second dimension of the typology reflects the degree of competence of the subsidiary itself, in terms of technology, production, marketing and management. This acknowledges the importance of strategic potentials at this level, so that Bartlett and Ghoshal indicate that if such subsidiaries are routinely relegated to implementing or adopting global directives of the parent group it will risk 'grossly under-utilising the company's worldwide assets and organisational capabilities'.

From the point of view of our concerns here the key quadrant of the Bartlett and Ghoshal typology is the *strategic leader*, which has a high level of in-house competences and operates in a location which itself has high strategic importance. It will have sensed new opportunities from the market and/or technologies accessible in the host economy and have internalised the capabilities to tailor its own competitive positioning from them. Bartlett and Ghoshal (1986, 80) indicate that it 'serves as a partner of headquarters in developing and implementing strategy' and generates its own distinctive resource base and competences to assert its position.

More analytically challenging is Bartlett and Ghoshal's *contributor*, which occupies the quadrant of high-level subsidiary capacities but is located in an economy of low strategic importance. Thus here idiosyncratic circumstances may have provided a subsidiary with an R&D-base and a level of technological competence that exceeds that possessed by other operations in other countries with similarly limited strategic relevance. Then 'rather than allowing these capacities to atrophy, or be dissipated in solving strategically irrelevant local problems, they should be co-opted into contributing specialised inputs to projects of corporate importance' (Papanastassiou and Pearce, 1999, 34). The KS contributions of such a contributor subsidiary are then more likely to diffuse into support of creative work elsewhere in the MNE group. This would then question the value of such subsidiaries to the longer-term development of the host country; the MNEs generate knowledge there but are likely to use it productively elsewhere.

The most clearly articulated position for ES in the Bartlett and Ghoshal typology is the *implementer* with 'just enough competence' to sustain its operations in a market of low strategic importance. They function as 'deliverers of the company's value added' by focusing on effective supply of existing goods and providing 'the opportunity to capture economies of scale and scope that are crucial to most companies' global strategies' (Bartlett and Ghoshal, 1986, 91). However, in terms of intra-group competitive evolution, Bartlett and Ghoshal note that prolonged subsidiary-level emphasis on such an ES focus on low cost could consign it to the *black hole* categorisation of subsidiaries with low competences in a market of high strategic importance. Myopic decision making between a subsidiary and HQ management may lead to persistence of an inappropriate focus on ES. It may fail to adequately perceive that the host-country development has moved forward in ways that now render low-cost supply a less viable strategy. Then it may also fail to detect those new subsidiary-level upgrading potentials that should be endemic to responding to such progress.

To complete this section we can invoke another, differently positioned, typology offered by Bartlett and Ghoshal (1989, 1990). Here they acknowledge the group-level acceptance of decentralised innovation in MNEs and present four different ways that this had been positioned and structured. Two of these approaches are seen as *traditional* and reflect relatively limited perspectives on the acceptance of integrated and interdependent international strategies. The two *transnational* approaches do then reflect a refocused positioning of innovation within the much more diverse and interactive global strategies implied by such overall organisational structures.

The first traditional approach is categorised as *centre-for-global*. This perceives total responsibility for innovation as being centralised in the home country, with the innovated products then available to be exploited in the group's markets worldwide. Though this carries some resonances with the first stage of Vernon's PLCM there are, in fact, key differences. For Vernon the enforced centralised innovation created the competitive advantages that then allowed the firm to become an MNE and, as we argued, this could then soon lead to newly diversified KS perspectives leading to a degree of decentralised innovation. By contrast the centre-for-global approach is seen as a considered and dogmatic centralised decision made by a firm that is already an MNE, and which disallows any attempts to interject differentiating behaviour from implementing subsidiaries. The merit of centralisation is that it could 'create new products and processes at relatively low cost and high speed' (Bartlett and Ghoshal, 1989, 58) and benefit from the retention of vital competences at the parent unit so as to protect them administratively and achieve economies of scale and specialisation in, especially, R&D. In its extreme form the centre-for-global approach can now be seen as problematically insensitive, as it excluded any subsidiary-level adaptation of the centrally created goods in ways that could be responsive to local conditions and enhance competitive effectiveness. Bartlett and Ghoshal suggest that trying to build this degree of responsive product differentiation into a still centrally dominated innovation approach would have failed. Thus 'even when diverse local needs are understood, the central response can be inappropriate because of either over-specification that tries to satisfy all the demands, or a grand compromise that satisfies none' (Bartlett and Ghoshal, 1989, 58–9).

The second traditional approach to innovation is *local-for-local* which Bartlett and Ghoshal (1990, 317) describe as one where 'national subsidiaries of MNCs [use] their own resources and capabilities to create innovations that respond to the needs of their own environments'. It is an extreme form of fragmented decentralised innovation and can be seen as a manifestation of MS subsidiary behaviour in, retrospectively, a dangerously dysfunctional format of a multi-domestic hierarchy. Its obvious strength, of course, is that it precisely negates the systemic rejection of local responsiveness in centre-for-global with an equally dogmatic focus on local needs and conditions that permits distinctive competitiveness there. The weaknesses of the local-for-local approach had manifested themselves both in terms of inefficiencies at the group level, in terms of integration and coordination, and in sustainability at the subsidiary level.

The lack of group-level oversight may have led to wasteful duplication of efforts between subsidiaries and an extensive redundancy in resource application that would result in diminished returns to the use of the group's overall (but incoherently fragmented) creative resources. The other consequence of the fragmentation of innovation into subsidiaries with mainly local-market-focused objectives – and with inevitably constrained budgets – is that it severely limits the scope for serious commitment to the expensive and risky forms of precompetitive (scientifically and exploratory) basic research that are needed to build the scopes for more path-breaking medium- and long-term product development. An argued strength of the centre-for-global approach was that by centralising the research budgets it could afford to address these types of speculative exploratory R&D. Ultimately, in the local-for-local approach the lack of context for these types of research would leave subsidiaries trying to squeeze more innovations out of a, more or less fixed, stock of core technology, with the aggregate result of stagnating innovation potentials at the group level.

It can then be seen that the two transnational approaches described by Bartlett and Ghoshal sought 'to harness proactively to group-level competitiveness those differences in international environments (diversity of consumer needs, market trends, technological breakthroughs and governmental demands) that tended to prove so problematical to traditional modes of innovation' (Papanastassiou and Pearce, 1999, 97). Both the transnational approaches seek to address the scope economies that become available to MNEs through the systematic international learning processes of a KS strategic orientation. These approaches 'are based on the ability to leverage existing innovative resources and capabilities by capturing synergies in their combined application or gaining scale and scope economies through broader exploitation of innovation' (Bartlett and Ghoshal, 1990, 248).

Here the *locally leveraged* approach to innovation utilises a subsidiary's access to distinctive host-country creative resources and insights to create new products whose originality can be exploited in the group's international markets. This can be seen, to some degree, as a strategic repositioning of the local-for-local approach in that it once again draws a set of locally accessed creative resources into a fully completed innovation that is coordinated within the subsidiary itself. But now this is also fully comprehended and mandated by the parent group, which sees it as positioned within an integrated and coherent global innovation strategy (Papanastassiou and Pearce, 2009, Chapter 8). This should eliminate redundancies between innovation-oriented subsidiaries and, instead, organise supportive knowledge transfers between them as appropriate. Such an approach should also aim to secure adequate provision for precompetitive R&D in the group. This is still unlikely to be performed to any degree in such subsidiaries, but now there may be a centrally supported set of such laboratories in appropriate locations and their emerging insights can be made available to the support of innovative subsidiaries as and when needed. This will be elaborated in the next section on types of R&D units. In effect the locally leveraged approach to innovation is the responsibility of product mandate subsidiaries or Bartlett and Ghoshal's strategic leaders. It also retains the persisting emphasis on the value of the strong inter-functional, but intra-subsidiary, communications asserted by Vernon for innovation in the first phase of the PLCM. But it now also emphasises the value of escaping from total introversion in the process, encouraging such subsidiaries to both access supportive knowledge from elsewhere in the group and to make their own expertise similarly available.

The second transnational approach was seen by Bartlett and Ghoshal as much more speculative but as providing a more complete means of drawing diverse and dispersed creative assets into an effective innovation. This *globally linked* approach addressed the potentials to be gained from building an innovation around inputs from a range of different facilities in different locations. This could involve several R&D labs experimenting in different areas of science, market research in a range of culturally diverse countries, a number of potentially inventive engineering groups and the oversight of a coordinating unit that need not necessarily be in the home country of the MNE (though still likely to be ultimately responsible to it). Whereas the locally leveraged approach works for the *group* as a coherent means of securing a range of different innovations from different subsidiaries, the globally linked approach seeks to decentralise the inputs to a single *innovation* itself. In the locally leveraged approach the clearly understood benefits of strong inter-functional communications in a single unit may hide a significant limitation. The chosen location may not provide the most effective available inputs in *all* the relevant functional areas. Whilst it may be the best available single location *overall*, achievement may still be compromised by a certain degree of substandard input in one or more functions. The inculcation of knowledge exchanges between units in this approach to innovation, noted above, may be a partial and rather ad hoc recognition of this constraint. What the globally linked approach would aspire to do would then be to take these knowledge interdependencies to its logical extreme, by trying to assemble an ideal mix of the best available inputs to address all the separate investigative and creative needs of a single innovation. The reason why this approach was only provisionally articulated by Bartlett and Ghoshal was the obvious one that the difficulty and costs of achieving the needed levels of subtle and speculative communication necessary for innovation in such a dispersed (geographically and culturally) network would be prohibitive. Even with the massive improvements in international communication technologies since Bartlett and Ghoshal's research this may still leave the full viability of globally linked innovations in doubt. There may still be a difficult trade-off between the benefits of full access to dispersed specialisations in innovative competences and the costs of securing the degrees of intimate communications needed to fully realise the interactive subtleties of their combination in one innovation.

DECENTRALISATION OF R&D IN MNEs

It is central to the arguments of this chapter that the systematic adoption of knowledge seeking by MNEs provided a crucial impetus to their organisational restructuring in recent decades. Yet it is also quite notable that the two key aspects of KS that we focus on here emerged from quite different origins in the literature and that the logically inherent practical interdependencies between them took some time to be fully recognised. Indeed, the initial 'discovery' of these emergent areas of analysis came from quite different methodological sources. We have placed the roots of the discussion of subsidiary-level innovation, as an emerging practice, in MNEs in a number of Canadian case studies.

By contrast the realisation (against a pronounced received wisdom) that dispersal of R&D by MNEs was a non-negligible phenomenon and worthy of analysis came from the publication of industry-level data for US companies.[4] This provided an impetus towards pioneering studies that focused on *empirical* tests of aggregate industry-[5] or firm-level[6] R&D-expenditure data.

In retrospect it can be seen that the early modelling of decentralised R&D in MNEs placed this mostly within the decision parameters of our multi-domestic hierarchy and its MS strategies. Thus the prevalent implicit perspective was that where it occurred the purpose of overseas R&D would be to support in a direct fashion the short-term needs of individual production subsidiaries, usually with the aim of improving their ability to be competitive in their host-country market. The total amount of decentralised R&D that emerged in a particular MNE would then reflect the number and size of subsidiaries that felt they could benefit from an in-house R&D unit and that were then able to convince the parent company, in a bilateral bargaining process, that the establishment of such a facility would support overall group interests. Beyond this fragmented and ad hoc set of negotiations there was no sense at this stage of MNEs having an overarching global R&D strategy into which separate units could fit in systemic group-supporting ways.

Consequently, the broad approach adopted in this 'first wave' of empirical studies saw an MNE as determining 'the location of its R&D by reconciling centripetal and centrifugal forces' (Hirschey and Caves, 1981, 117). Here certain factors might enable an individual subsidiary to pull some R&D work into its operations. However, this was usually perceived as being achieved against a natural group-level 'gravitational force' which generated a predominant momentum towards the retention of the more strategically creative (and more expensive) work at the centre. Using a dependent variable that was usually defined as the proportion of total R&D carried out outside the industry or firm's home country, these studies then tested potential determinants in terms of their likely contribution to the decentralising (centrifugal) or centralising (centripetal) forces operating in MNE R&D.

The pervasive perspective in these 'first wave' studies was that the dominant centrifugal force likely to induce overseas R&D in such multi-domestic hierarchies would be the need to adapt the product or process technology transferred from the parent company to a subsidiary's local market and production conditions. Thus variables were usually included to measure the share of overseas sales or production in the total group sales, to serve as a proxy for the strength of this decentralising force. These studies provided near consensus that higher levels of overseas sales/production in MNEs were a significant positive determinant of higher shares of overseas R&D in overall R&D expenditures (Mansfield et al., 1979; Hirschey and Caves, 1981; Lall, 1979; Pearce, 1989, 60–7, 71–89; Håkanson, 1981).[7]

Two strongly interrelated factors provided the core of the centripetal/centralising forces argued in the early analyses of R&D in MNEs. These were the importance of economies of scale in the efficient location of R&D and the role and nature of communications and coordination in securing its effective implementation.

The economies of scale argument assumed, in essence, that the implementation of additional, geographically dispersed, R&D units would only be considered to be an economically viable proposition when the first, probably parent or home-country, laboratory had achieved a 'critical mass' so that it was making full use of all its resources (Pearce, 1989, 38). By way of illustration we can suggest two types of R&D resource whose large capacities may underpin the 'critical mass' or economies of scale view. The first is the perceived need for R&D personnel to comprise balanced *teams* of scientific specialists. This could put upward pressure on the minimum efficient level of activity in a central laboratory by, firstly, requiring a large team in order to encompass all relevant areas of specialised expertise and, secondly, to then provide enough work to fully employ such specialists in the use of their unique and distinctive capability.

The second fixed-resource case could be the acquisition of a piece of expensive high-capacity research equipment by the central laboratory, which might then focus all R&D programmes onto this unit until it is being optimally utilised. The 'indivisibility' influences on economies of scale in R&D might then be reinforced by 'learning by doing' arguments, where the central laboratory's effective capacity could be seen to grow over time as the research teams settle down and better understand their integral competences and also increase their familiarity with available advanced equipment.[8]

However, we can now suggest that whilst economies of scale might well have been a force initially restraining the start of R&D decentralisation in MNEs its influence would quickly decline once a system of dispersed facilities did emerge. Thus sharing of specialised assets (equipment or the expertise of personnel) in interdependent R&D networks can lessen the economies of scale impact of apparent indivisibilities. For instance, if the factor that seemed to set a high minimum efficient scale of a central laboratory's activity was an expensive and high-capacity piece of equipment, then the emergence of sister laboratories elsewhere in the MNE group could secure the full use of this equipment by making it available to projects that are generated and substantially executed in those other units. It would then be no longer necessary to expand the in-house work of the central laboratory (in a way that was originally assumed to, in effect, crowd-out the possibility of other units overseas) to achieve optimal use of its indivisible asset.[9]

However, if sharing of indivisible resources and project mobility within an MNE's R&D network provides a potential escape route from economies of scale as a centripetal force, the benefits of such interdependencies 'may only be perceived where knowledge of the ongoing work and capabilities within the dispersed network is effectively diffused and assimilated' (Pearce, 1989, 39). Securing the network benefits depends not only on the existence of decentralised laboratories but also on an effective communications network and a culture of mutually supportive cooperation between these dispersed units. Though we can now argue that the inculcation of such a collaborative culture and supporting mechanisms needed to become innate to the implementation of strategy in heterarchy or transnational MNEs, it can also be understood why communications issues were discerned as operating in parallel with economies of scale as centralising forces in the earlier forms.

We can, in fact, now discern two contexts for understanding communications as an influence on R&D decentralisation and networking in MNEs. The fact that early analyses tended to implicitly interpret this as a constraining problem may actually have merely reflected the presumed limited context for such knowledge transfers. Here the multi-domestic hierarchy perspective saw R&D laboratories as mainly oriented to secure effective one-way transfer of technology into subsidiaries, whose only concern was to assimilate it and apply it responsively to their isolated domestic competitive situation. This becomes the support laboratory (SL) role in the typology we will introduce later. But, as we have already suggested, communications did not operate as a constraint once MNE strategies required more intricate and subtle international information transfers. Once required to do so these companies proved able to generate effective communications between R&D units located in different countries (or regions), allowing for the more ambitious aims of securing synergistic benefits from an ability to leverage each of their distinctive creative competences to group-level needs and aims.

The second context relates to the perceived communications benefits from the co-location of R&D with other key functions in an innovation process that was, in early theorising, generally considered to be centralised in the firm's country of origin. This is, of course, the approach to innovation presented by Vernon (1966) in the first stage of his PLCM. Except, however, that since he placed strong emphasis on the innovation process being market-driven he did not draw out the specific implications for R&D to any systematic degree. Lall (1979, 322–4) subsequently achieved this. Firstly, Lall argues that in many industries (he emphasises engineering in particular) it is difficult to 'delink' R&D, due to a 'need for continuous interaction between all the major innovative functions and procurement, management and marketing functions' (Lall, 1979, 323). Secondly, since the home country of an MNE (the US in Lall's model, as for much early theorising) provides both the location of the main decision-making centre and the market that provides the initial impetus to the product development process, the benefits of inter-functional communications also constrains innovation-oriented R&D to this central location.

This view of considerable benefits from close and effective inter-functional communications in securing the efficient completion of a particular innovation has persisted into the modelling of innovation in the more heterarchical and strategically dispersed MNEs. But with the crucial proviso that now, in such MNEs, the possibility for such integrated and self-contained innovation has migrated from exclusive centrality to a number of dispersed locations. A crucial factor in driving this, or at least not constraining it, is the scope for acquiring strong and distinctive R&D inputs in these locations; this form of communications interdependencies remains relevant but no longer constrains R&D decentralisation. So we can now see decentralisation of R&D as decisively integral to the effective operation of product mandate subsidiaries and to the activation of Bartlett and Ghoshal's locally leveraged approach to innovation. In terms of the typology of R&D units this becomes a locally integrated laboratory (LIL), operating in a systematically integrated fashion with other local innovation-oriented functions to support a product development process at the subsidiary level.

Though we have placed the determinants of the centralisation versus decentralisation decision for MNE R&D firmly within the context of the MS priorities of the multi-domestic hierarchy, some of these first-wave studies did explore the possible implications of other subsidiary-level roles. Indeed, we can, at least tentatively, interpolate some of these results as pointing towards implications of MNEs' strategic evolution beyond such bases.

In their study Hirschey and Caves (1981, 119) test the variable 'foreign affiliates' exports to destinations other than the US divided by total sales by foreign affiliates'. This variable, using their 1966 US data, emerged as consistently and significantly related to the proportion of R&D overseas. However, when Pearce (1989, 60–7) tested the 1982 US data the result was persistently negatively signed (though mainly short of significance). This, Pearce (1989, 66) suggests, was likely to reflect MNEs' increasing capacity to *select* locations for ES export-oriented subsidiaries, so that input availabilities and productive capacities were carefully matched to the technologies to be used. This would rule out the need for locally adaptive R&D in such subsidiaries. By contrast, in 1966, the firms might have been forced to realise economies of scale in export-oriented production from initially technologically inappropriate locations, generating the need for process adaptive R&D. A factor contributing to such a biased location decision, in the essentially more protected trading environment of the 1960s, might have been that the locations available for such low-cost trade-related production were limited to a few with access to preferential trade arrangements.

In their tests of the R&D intensity of subsidiaries' operations as an alternative dependent variable Papanastassiou and Pearce (1997), Zejan (1990) and Kumar (1996) all used a variant of the export-ratio as a potential determinant.[10] The dominant result for Papanastassiou and Pearce and Zejan was a positive relationship between export orientation and

R&D intensity. The logical interpretation of this, we can now see, would be the presence of product development in PM-type subsidiaries. This, of course, does not imply that across the board PMs had come to dominate the exporting behaviour of these subsidiaries. More plausibly it is likely that product development activity in subsidiaries, where it is present, is much more research intensive than local-market operations and generates significantly more valuable exports than ES operations which may also have low research intensity.[11]

By contrast with these two studies Kumar's (1996) test of pooled US data for 1977, 1982 and 1989, provided insignificant negative results for a full sample and an industrialised-country subsample, with this relationship becoming significant for the developing-country subsample. For the first two samples Kumar (1996, 681) says 'it appears that export-oriented affiliates produce largely to the designs supplied to them by parents [so that] R&D facilities for supporting them are not necessary'. For the developing-country subsample he argues (Kumar, 1996, 682) 'that affiliate R&D in developing countries whenever undertaken is geared towards adaptations for the local market', in effect confirming a below-average need for adaptation in cost-competitive export ES behaviour. The absence of the signs of PM behaviour, as suggested by Papanastassiou and Pearce and Zejan, may reflect the presence of relatively early (1977, 1982) data in the pooled samples. It may also be that the insignificance of the negative result for developed countries (compared to significant for developing countries) could reflect the emergence of some R&D-intensive product development in these more advanced subsidiaries.

We can see now that this last set of results pointed towards two clear implications for the further investigation of the role of decentralising R&D in the wider strategic evolution of MNEs. As the previous discussion has suggested the need for subsidiary-level R&D would be likely to vary according to whether its role was MS (need to adapt goods to the local market), ES (ideally very little need for process adaptation) or KS (R&D as a key input into product development). The second implication was that the types of quantitative data used in the first-wave studies could only provide speculative interpretations along these lines of the emerging strategic diversity within MNEs and its reflection at the subsidiary level. The logical impetus was thus towards what we can designate as a 'second wave' of qualitative survey-based studies. The objective became to address, through the responses of practitioners, the complexities and subtleties of MNEs' increasing commitment to decentralised R&D as a core component of evolving global competitive strategies. With all the accepted compromises of survey (or case study) methodology, this allowed researchers to attempt to draw out the varied nuances of the positioning of MNE R&D in a manner not available to the data-driven aggregates of the first wave.

In fact two remarkable pioneering survey studies *had* ventured into the unknown territory of the organisational and strategic diversity of R&D in MNEs alongside the earliest of the first-wave empirical analyses. Indeed we can now see that these studies introduced two of the key concerns of the later 'mainstream' second-wave surveys. Firstly, Ronstadt (1977, 1978) provides a typology of the potential roles that decentralised R&D laboratories might play in securing both the current and future competitiveness of their MNE groups. Secondly, Behrman and Fischer (1980a, 1980b) address the complementary issue of how the extent and nature of such R&D units would be related to the wider strategic organisation and objectives of their parent group. Despite their exploratory nature and positioning in the early phases of the phenomenon itself, it is these studies that we elaborate here to exemplify the indicative foundations of the subsequent wave of survey analyses.

Ronstadt surveyed the R&D abroad of seven US MNEs in 1974, and obtained evidence on 55 overseas laboratories in these companies. Of these 49 were still operative at the time of his investigation, with the other six having been closed. In terms of their origins 42 of these laboratories had been created as new units by a decision of the MNE, whilst 13 had been acquired as part of firms taken over by the MNE.

The most prevalent of the four roles that Ronstadt distinguished among these laboratories was the *technology transfer unit* (TTU). The purpose of TTU was to help the subsidiaries to transfer manufacturing technology from the US parent and then to provide technical services for foreign customers. Of the laboratories that had been set up as new by the MNEs, 31 (74 per cent) were initiated as TTUs, though by 1974 only 17 of them continued to play that role, with 12 having acceded to more ambitious roles and two closed. Of the acquired units, six (46 per cent) were effectively TTUs, this reflecting the fact that the firms taken over were already accessing and using the MNE's technology in a licensing arrangement.

This dominant positioning of TTUs reflects perfectly what early theorising could have anticipated in the still hierarchically centralised MNEs of that time. This would assume overseas manufacturing subsidiaries that are still dependent on competitive capacities (OAs) created and transferred by parent companies, with market conditions in host countries the key motivation (LAs) determining this.[12] Also the TTU role matches the underlying assumptions indicating the main decentralising forces that were to be tested in the pioneering empirical studies. However, the second major contribution of Ronstadt's study was to accept the likelihood that decentralised R&D operations could become an influential component of the internal dynamics of subsidiaries and the wider organisational restructuring of MNEs. Even at this early stage, he was finding, the TTU could be a transitory role with potential to move on to more locally individualising functions.

The most immediately influential of these localising roles was the *indigenous technology unit* (ITU), which aimed to develop new and/or improved products expressly for overseas markets and to do so in ways that meant the new products were *not* dependent on access to new technology supplied by the parent. By 1974 Ronstadt found that 11 of the 42 laboratories that had been founded by the MNEs were playing the ITU role; two of which had been established to play that role and nine that had evolved into it from an initial TTU status. Also seven of the 13 units that had been acquired by MNEs appeared to be already playing ITU roles in the firm taken over. It is not clear whether this in-place innovative capacity was a direct motivation for the local firm's acquisition.

Ronstadt's interviews suggested several ways in which the emergence of ITUs reflected distinctive individualising ambitions in subsidiaries. These took forms that would become familiar in later analyses of MNE organisational dynamics, but which were still alien to most of the persisting assumptions of hegemonic hierarchy. On what we now consider the *demand*-side, Ronstadt suggested that subsidiary managers advocating ITU support had begun to doubt the parent company's capacity to provide the persistent stream of new products and processes that would allow them to sustain their desired rate of growth in their domestic market. On the *supply*-side, Ronstadt found that managers were increasingly able to identify, in their local economy, new or distinctively different investment opportunities and to project to the parent company their managerial and technical capacity to independently carry out such new product developments.

Where these ITUs evolved from TTU origins Ronstadt found two sources of internal dynamics that pointed towards the logic of this subsidiary-level upgrading. Firstly, the laboratory's directors felt the need to provide more challenging work so that they could keep their best personnel and recruit additional high-quality R&D specialists. This again reflects the growing supply-side perception of some host countries' ability to provide distinctive knowledge inputs to MNEs' competitive development. Secondly, the subsidiaries' general and marketing managers perceived the need to move from TTU to ITU demand-side ambitions, because the individualising product potentials they targeted would assert stronger competitive status within the group. Overall, the positioning of ITU remained one of strengthening the subsidiary's status in its host-country market, perhaps through the approach to innovation designated as local-for-local by Bartlett and Ghoshal. The two remaining, much more speculative, and empirically tentative, types of laboratories offered by Ronstadt do then point towards positions in rather differently configured MNE structures.

Firstly, the *global technology unit* (GTU) was established to develop new products and processes for more or less simultaneous application in the parent MNE's global markets. In Ronstadt's original research GTUs were a very specialised case since he only found them in IBM, which reported eight cases in 1974. Five of these had been set up as GTUs and three had grown into the role having started as TTUs and then moved through an intermediate status as ITUs. Nevertheless, despite their contextual limitation in 1974, we can find several perceptive forward-looking possibilities in Ronstadt's GTUs. Thus it was suggested that once MNEs had begun to allocate different *production* responsibilities to different subsidiaries as part of an integrated global supply network there would then be benefits to allowing individual operations to develop their own product. This initially takes us into the world of the ES network hierarchy of integrated specialist supply subsidiaries but then moves it forward to such subsidiaries asserting a position in what could become Bartlett and Ghoshal's locally leveraged innovation process. Two sources of the latter potential were suggested. Firstly, a subsidiary that is well embedded in the potentials of its host economy may detect the scope for assembling the range of functional competences seen as necessary to secure effective innovation. Secondly, a globally oriented MNE that is working towards a major new *range* of products for its markets may feel the need to decentralise work (including R&D) in support of this because none of its locations could supply all the research resources needed at the required quality or specialisation.

Finally, the *corporate technology unit* (CTU) sought to generate new technology of a long-term or exploratory nature expressly for the parent MNE group. Though this role places the CTU, like the GTU, in a global programme that is initiated and overseen by the group parent its objectives are very different. Whereas the GTU was positioned to pursue a fairly clearly defined innovation the CTU explores, through basic scientific research, the precompetitive need to generate new technologies that could, further down the road, feed into major new innovations. For the first time in the typology the CTU operates in isolation from other innovation-oriented functions and, in practice, prefers to operate on a standalone basis away from facilities more directly concerned with current competitiveness. Ronstadt found that four of the 42 units set up by MNEs were initiated as CTUs, but that this had proved a very vulnerable status. Two of these had been disbanded by 1974, as they were not seen to be providing useful results. The other two seemed to be in the process of being refocused towards more immediately innovation-supporting roles, with elements of ITU or GTU responsibilities. Nevertheless, as we will see, the types of positioning envisaged for Ronstadt's CTU did become a significant component of subsequent R&D diversity in MNEs.

The work of Behrman and Fischer (1980a, 1980b) complements that of Ronstadt by placing the extent and nature of overseas R&D in MNEs within the widening strategic diversity of these firms. To do this Behrman and Fischer categorised the 50 US and European MNEs they investigated in terms of three overarching strategic priorities. In a way that would reflect the persistence of the MS motivation, in what we have termed the multi-domestic hierarchy, the most prevalent of the MNE types that Behrman and Fischer analysed were designated as having a *host-market* orientation, with subsidiaries predominantly intended to supply their domestic market.

Reflecting the results of the first-wave empirical studies and Ronstadt's delineation of TTUs the expectation here would be that low-level R&D laboratories could often play a role in adapting products and processes to local tastes and conditions. In line with this, the 23 host-market US MNEs in the Behrman and Fischer survey reported 96 foreign R&D operations (i.e. 5.87 per MNE). Further information on the 96 US MNE facilities did confirm that their mainstream activity was locally responsive adaptation. However, Behrman and Fischer (1980a, 17; 1980b, 57) also reported that 25 of these US host-market laboratories included some 'new product research' and two extended their horizons to 'exploratory research'. Once again evidence was clearly emerging of the potentials for evolutionary deepening in laboratories that started with very limited adaptive roles within the core technologies of such MNEs.

Alternatively for Behrman and Fischer *home-market* MNEs continued to expect their overseas subsidiaries to occupy very much secondary roles, oriented to support the primacy of the home-countries' operations and aims. This could include the resource-seeking (RS) role of supplying raw materials, or variants of efficiency seeking such as providing the parent company with particular component parts or performing a specialised stage in a vertically integrated production process organised by the parent. The restriction of the output of these subsidiaries to predetermined intermediate goods or commodities would normally rule out subsidiary-level product adaptation and limit any process adaptive role for R&D to marginal adjustments to production (or extraction or agricultural processes) to accommodate local conditions. In fact, Behrman and Fischer only located seven such home-market MNEs, all of US origin. This may reflect the relative retreat of the RS role and the limited embrace by that time of the (Japanese pioneered) ES role by Western MNEs. Furthermore, these seven MNEs only possessed three R&D units (that is, 0.43 per MNE) in total with none of these extending beyond the limited adaptive responsibilities suggested into either 'new product research' or 'exploratory research' (Behrman and Fischer, 1980a, 17; 1980b, 57).

Finally, Behrman and Fischer introduce, perhaps more speculatively, the *world-market* MNE. These were seen to integrate their foreign affiliates into centrally coordinated programmes to serve standardised world markets. As we now understand the emerging strategic postures of 1970s MNEs these world-market companies could have already embodied very diverse roles for their subsidiaries. Firstly, they would logically include what we would now consider the more conventional networked mode of ES behaviour; as distinct from the centre-supplying variant they postulated for the home-market MNE. As already argued, these types of subsidiary responsibilities would rarely provoke any significant need for R&D support. Secondly, they could already have been starting to embrace the KS roles of subsidiary-level innovation and creative activities. This would then certainly be providing the need for R&D units with capabilities well beyond the limited adaptation expected in the earlier MNE formulations.[13]

Behrman and Fischer in fact only found five world-market MNEs; four from the US, one from Europe, with all except one in electronics-related industries. Though this does suggest that few of Behrman and Fischer's respondents saw global networking of their operations as their dominant mode of operating by the late 1970s their R&D results do reflect interestingly on evolutionary potentials that seemed to be emerging.[14] The four US world-market MNEs had only seven overseas R&D laboratories (that is, 1.75 per MNE), which would suggest the dominance of the ES role overall. But of these seven laboratories five included 'new product research' and three also carried out 'exploratory research'. This indicates that, where it occurs, the R&D in world-market MNEs is much more decisively targeting creative and innovation-oriented work than in the other types of MNEs studied. The presence of KS at the subsidiary level did seem to be coming into focus in such MNEs. The one European world-market MNE possessed 12 R&D units, but their roles and strategic positioning was not reported.

Despite their substantial validation of the mainstream presumptions of the 'first wave' of empirical studies the distinctive value of the two pioneering survey analyses lay in the way they pointed towards the potentials for dispersed R&D operations to play more important roles in the differentiating dynamics of MNEs' strategic evolution. To embrace and document these new scopes and roles a 'second wave' of surveys looked at MNEs' R&D across a variety of home- and host-country contexts and industrial sectors. We can now suggest that these studies came to indicate four ways in which the repositioning of overseas R&D, within the wider strategic evolution of MNEs, differentiated itself from the limited and centralised hierarchical dependency of the earlier perspectives.

The first of these changes was that, on what we have designated as the *demand*-side, the defining motivation for such R&D moved from *adaptation* to *development*. What the MNEs required from such operations evolved from merely securing the most effective application of extant technologies and products in a multiplicity of separate host-country competitive contexts to a contribution towards the more globally structured need to regenerate this product range and reinforce the technologies that could underpin it. This strategic repositioning of such R&D in fact points towards the second change. When the role was constrained to multi-domestic adaptation the work would inevitably be done in the MS subsidiary supplying that market. The presumption of subsidiary-level development, however, was that any goods created would target a much wider range of markets in the MNE. The location for such subsidiaries and their development-oriented R&D laboratories could be anywhere in the relevant (regional or global) market.

Thus *supply*-side factors would become decisively relevant. This then contextualises the emergence of KS as a distinct motivation in MNEs. Whilst the globalising of markets, notably those for newly innovated goods and services, re-emphasised development as a vital competitive strategy, it also opened up to MNEs the careful consideration of *where* to locate such operations: our supply-side factors. The ability to detect and leverage distinctive creative inputs (including, but not limited to, R&D capabilities) from *particular* locations *towards* globalised innovation and knowledge enhancement become central to the new (heterarchical/transnational) structure of MNEs.

The third change detected was from the *independence* of local-market adaptation (albeit *dependence* on mature group technologies) to the *interdependencies* of R&D laboratories' positioning in MNEs' KS strategic programmes. Here it was suggested (Papanastassiou and Pearce, 1998) that this would become an example of the organisational challenges of 'interdependent individualism' in these new organisational forms. The laboratories (or, in other contexts, subsidiaries) should be encouraged to generate *individualised* competences from their host-country knowledge base, but to allow for the leveraging of these *interdependently* into wider group programmes.

Finally, the results indicated a further weakening of the centralising forces presumed by the first-wave framework. Two forces may have provoked this decline. Firstly, a *need* to overcome them in view of the increasing strength and awareness of the competitive benefits of integrating decentralised attributes into strategic global programmes of KS operations. Secondly, the *ability* to secure these benefits that become increasingly available with improved means of communication and coordination.

To draw these themes into a synoptic view of the status of decentralised R&D in the strategic diversity of the current heterarchical or transnational MNE we can revert to the idea of a typology of laboratory roles.[15] The varied assertions just outlined, regarding the distinctive characteristics of R&D in MNEs, then provide us with a number of questions to be posed of each of the laboratory types. What role does it play in the wider competitive needs and aims of the MNE group? What types of subsidiary, if any, does this lead it to be associated with? Is its role mainly demand-side or supply-side driven, and what are the defining elements of such influences? In what ways is the laboratory likely to be integrated into group-level knowledge exchanges, beyond those within any subsidiary it is part of?

We start with the simplest, and logically earliest, type of overseas unit the *support laboratory* (SL), whose main objective (as with Ronstadt's TTU) was to facilitate effective transfer of mature technologies within the MNE group. In its original formulation the SL thus addressed 'the most traditional centrifugal influence in the form of support for the improved decentralised application of an MNE's established (and probably centrally created) technology as already embodied in its current products' (Papanastassiou and Pearce, 1999, 149). This clearly positions these SLs as integral to the types of subsidiaries whose role is constrained to the effective competitive application of these core products and technologies.[16] This would be most obviously the case in MS operations that open up the need to adapt the products and/or processes to distinctive local conditions. At most, a well-positioned ES operation should need minimal process adjustments. This indicated a demand-side role, in the sense that where an MNE accepts the need for a SL this will be because the subsidiary's competitive situation will benefit from its work. The associated presumption would, therefore, be that where these demand-side forces determine the need for SL work the level of expertise required would be quite easy to recruit and train. The essence of the SL role is the hierarchical exploitation of MNEs' current sources of competitiveness. It does this at a subsidiary-specific level, with no mandated expectation of any contribution to group-level competitiveness beyond its localised context; it is not, in and of itself, knowledge seeking.

The first decentralised laboratory role that does move beyond the exploitation of current sources of competitiveness, and into the explorative activities that are seeking to define new ones, has been designated as a *locally integrated laboratory* (LIL). This terminology serves to underline the two defining facets of these laboratories' positioning. Firstly, it participates in a subsidiary-level product development process that is *localised* in a particular host country, but with the objective of adding to the group's competitiveness in much more extensive market areas. It is part of Bartlett and Ghoshal's 'locally leveraged' transnational approach to innovation as part of subsidiaries that have product mandate or similar developmental responsibilities. Secondly, such an in-house R&D unit addresses these innovation responsibilities by working in a closely *integrated* manner with marketing personnel, engineering and ambitious subsidiary-level management. It retains Vernon's perception of the need for closely integrated inter-functional communication in an innovation process. The hope would be that the collaboration would 'ensure that a new good meets originally perceived market needs, can be effectively produced in local conditions and supports wider managerial views of the subsidiary's desired process of evolution' (Papanastassiou and Pearce, 1999, 156).

This LIL positioning can be seen to be subject to both demand-side and supply-side influences. It is certainly responding to a clearly defined demand-side competitive objective of the group, both in terms of the broadly perceived need for innovation and through a commitment to a specific development process whose plausible outputs are becoming increasingly clearly defined. But since the achievements of such a subsidiary-level innovation are expected to target a wide market area (at least regional, if not global) where it is located is open to group-level discretion. The ability of a subsidiary to access the necessary creative inputs from its host economy (supply-side factors) becomes central to its capacity to acquire and sustain such high-value-added responsibilities. The requirements for the LIL itself will be experienced scientists with an informed capacity to fully understand the new technologies integral to the innovation and able to communicate them to the other functional personnel. They are unlikely to be the path-breaking research scientists who themselves have discovered the new technologies capable of being core drivers of significant innovations.

These longer-term needs for more radical bases in innovation then became the province of our last type of facility, the *internationally interdependent laboratory* (IIL). These laboratories operate 'independently of any producing subsidiary in order to carry out basic and/or applied research as part of a wider programme of precompetitive R&D that is implemented and coordinated by the MNE group' (Papanastassiou and Pearce, 1999, 157). The speculative and precompetitive exploratory research undertaken by IILs aims to contribute to the reinforcement and regeneration of the MNE's core stock of scientific knowledge in ways that are in no sense determined or motivated by any currently in-play commercial objectives or needs. This means that an IIL's work has no systematic association with the immediate concerns of any type of subsidiary. Demand-side factors have no immediate implications for what an IIL does or where it does it. They are 'uniquely responsive to supply-side location factors in the form of the distinctive strengths of host-countries' current research capacity and accumulated technological heritage' (Papanastassiou and Pearce, 1999, 157). In the absence of inter-functional communications within subsidiaries the predominant interdependency of IILs is with similarly research-oriented units in other locations. Thus the supply-side imperatives of IILs would place them within a network of diverse precompetitive facilities that aim to tap into the best available sources of research experience and expertise in a range of potentially relevant but distinctively differentiated scientific disciplines. By locating IILs in a number of such national science bases the MNE seeks to generate, and organise coordinated exchanges between, facilities that access top-quality sources of scientific investigation in each of the areas of knowledge with the potential to feed into technological progress in its industry.

THE MODERN MNE: STRATEGIC DIVERSITY FOR GLOBAL COMPETITIVENESS

By the early 1980s, we can now argue, intuitive *practice* had begun to put into place all the aspects of strategic diversity that would be subsumed into the organisational structures soon to be articulated as heterarchy or the transnational. The essence of this was the acknowledgement of MNEs' need to fully accept the internationalised dimensions implicit in pursuit of both the distinctive *current* and *future* aspects of competitiveness. The first of these priorities can be provided with the *theoretical* clarity of a static optimisation decision. Here firms that possess operative and proven sources of competitive advantage (OAs) seek to disperse their international activation into the varied locations that can provide the productive inputs (positive LAs; static comparative advantage; level-2 resources) that match their technological requirements and optimise current performance. Though less amenable to a precise targeting of desired outputs, the broad parameters of MNEs' dynamic sources of future competitiveness can also be articulated within standard theoretical constructs. Thus the essential aim of this KS context is to secure the significant upgrading or substantive regeneration of the firm's operative sources of competitiveness (OAs). It seeks to do this through the detection, acquisition and assimilation of dispersed sources of knowledge and creative inputs internationally (level-3 resources; dynamic comparative advantages). Placing this KS scenario as a logically evolutionary progression we can find two potential roles in it for the firm's current OAs. Firstly, well-understood and proven technologies are likely to both inform the exploratory processes that investigate and evaluate possible additional or incremental new sources and provide the capacity to assimilate and effectively operationalise them. Secondly, the established managerial abilities to operate in a multiplicity of different knowledge environments and draw relevant ones into coherently integrated programmes is also likely to be a key group-level expertise.

In depicting the background to the emergence of their *transnational* organisational structure Bartlett and Ghoshal (1989, 18) observe that 'by the mid-1980s the forces of global integration, local differentiation and world-wide innovation had all become strong and compelling' so that to compete successfully a firm needed to simultaneously 'develop global competitiveness, multinational flexibility and world-wide learning capability'. Here the transnationals pursue *global competitiveness* through 'dispersed and interdependent assets and resources' and, for Bartlett and Ghoshal, pioneer the configuration of their worldwide resources as integrated networks. Whereas earlier formulations of MNEs had 'made a common assumption' that 'the subsidiary's role is local, limited to activities within its own environment' now their emphasis had turned to export-oriented links within ES globalised approaches to supply. This then becomes, for Bartlett and Ghoshal, a significant aspect of a complementary feature of transnationals, their *multinational flexibility*, which is manifest through differentiated and evolving subsidiary roles. Thus, alongside the newer ES role of exporting standardised products into global-supply networks, other subsidiaries could still play the more traditional one of the responsive supply of such goods predominantly to their local market (an adaptive MS imperative).

But in the diversity of their transnational Bartlett and Ghoshal accepted the relevance to MNEs of moving beyond exploitation of current capabilities into the exploration for new ones. This involved the pursuit of *worldwide learning* through the joint group-wide development and sharing of knowledge. As expressed by Papanastassiou and Pearce (1999, 48) 'this can take the form of subsidiaries that make use of leading-edge technology that is locally available in order to develop products that may be applied elsewhere in the group [so that] responsibility for a product is still centralised, but no longer in the home country'. This status, therefore, devolves to subsidiaries some elements of the strategic leadership previously accepted as innately centralised, so that it becomes 'a key attribute of the transnational that contrasts sharply with the uniformity of organisational roles in more traditional companies' (Bartlett and Ghoshal, 1989, 62).

This latter point takes us neatly into the world of *heterarchy* (Hedlund, 1986, 1993; Hedlund and Rolander, 1990; Birkinshaw, 1994) defined as entailing 'a geographical diffusion of core strategic activities and coordinating roles, a break with the notion of one uniform hierarchy of decisions as well as organisational positions, and an increased focus on normative control mechanisms' (Hedlund and Rolander, 1990, 15). From their detailed delineation of the characteristics of heterarchy Hedlund and Rolander (1990, 25–6) distil several perspectives that point directly to our emphasis on strategic diversification and KS imperatives.

A move away from a hierarchically dominant HQ is reflected in the presence of 'many centres of different kinds' where traditionally centralised functions became 'geographically diffused, and no dimension (product, country, function) [is] uniformly superordinate'. From this emerges 'a strategic role for foreign subsidiaries', but with this positioned 'for the corporation as a whole [so that] corporate level strategy has to be both formulated and implemented in a geographically scattered network'. Furthermore, this dispersion of key scopes requires a 'structure that is flexible over time' so that a functioning heterarchy 'does not worry too much about logical inconsistency' but will place more emphasis 'on practical coherence'. The organisational emphasis moves from dogmatic hegemony to a form of intuitive interactive pragmatism.

Reflecting this, the KS imperative in heterarchy encourages 'radical problem orientation, rather than starting from existing resources, or from competitive positions in narrow fields of business'. This should lead to 'action programmes for seeking and generating new firm-specific advantages through global spread'. Very relevant to our central concerns here Hedlund and Rolander (1990, 26) suggest that 'exploitation of given, home-country based advantages is emphasised in the theory of the MNE, but this should not entrap the MNE in its action'.

In Figure 7.1 we present a very simplified and stylised model of the contemporary MNE, depicting key elements of its strategic diversity (as manifest in subsidiary roles) and the way this now generates many and varied forms of intra-group transfers and interdependencies. From the earlier network hierarchy (NH) we retain two ES subsidiaries. This reflects the persistence of the core strategic imperative of accessing dispersed input (level-2) resources to optimise the effectiveness of current competitive capacities. Their role of supply of many export markets is again depicted. There is, however, one adjustment to the ES role here compared to its positioning in the NH. Now, with the parallel presence of KS subsidiaries, the sources of the technologies to be used in ES supply are potentially diversified beyond the earlier dependence on the home country alone. Thus we show the possibility that ES_1 may receive technology from, for example, KS_4 and ES_2 from KS_3. The background to these new sources of intra-group technology transfers will be elaborated further on. Despite the complication of this diversified range of sources of the technologies that can be applied by them the control and coordination of the operations of the ES plants

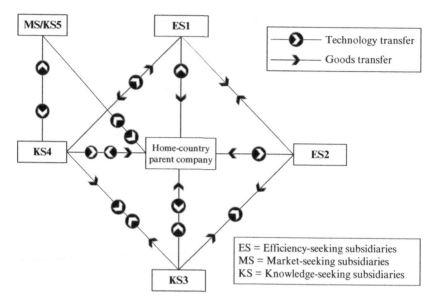

Figure 7.1   The strategically diverse multinational

themselves will remain essentially hierarchical and centralised. What each
one produces, in what quantities, and for which markets, remains a matter
of group-level decision making. This emphasises that one aspect of the
heterogeneity endemic to these MNEs lies in the need to adopt a mixture
of organisational approaches, tailored to secure the most effective performance of diverse strategic imperatives at the subsidiary level.

As indicated in the key emphases of this chapter, the crucial new strategic territory entered in the heterarchical/transnational organisational
structures was the dispersal into overseas operations of learning and creative priorities and processes. The figure addresses this through two KS
subsidiaries, with the ultimate objective of adding to the group's future
competitiveness through the development of new products and the expansion of its stock of technologies, knowledge and tacit expertise. The core
of the strategic positioning of those KS facilities is that of *interdependent
individualism* (Papanastassiou and Pearce, 1998), which provides them
with both inward- and outward-facing responsibilities. The first of these
is to *individualise* their position in the group through the generation of
distinctive subsidiary-level creative competences. The core of the ability
to do this would derive from detecting, accessing and internalising unique
elements of the host-country's science, technology and inventive human
capital. The most direct manifestation of this, for the group, would be the

development of significant new goods. But both achieving this innovation and its operationalisation for group competitiveness involves crucial *interdependencies*.

The first context for these interdependencies relates to the optimal completion of the product development process itself and also to the ability of a successful KS operation to contribute to the wider technological progress of its group, beyond its own immediate subsidiary-specific innovation concerns. Though the individualising essence of a successful subsidiary-level innovation should come from its locally accessed inputs it is unlikely to be either feasible or desirable that the process should be completed independently of supportive group interdependencies and of supplementary knowledge inputs from other group sources. Figure 7.1 depicts two-way flows of knowledge between both KS_3 and KS_4 and the home-country parent HQ. This accepts that the vast majority of successful subsidiary-level innovations will be evolutionary rather than revolutionary, in terms of their contribution to a coherent overall expansion of the group's globally operative product range. They will add very distinctive locally derived insights (technological, market-driven, engineering) to a platform of established competitive capacities, the broad comprehension of which is held by the parent company. Access to this as part of their own innovation projects is likely to be important to KS subsidiaries, both to supplement their own competences and to ensure that their developmental achievements are acceptable as viable components of their groups' competitive evolution. But securing such meaningful and useful flows of information from the parent to KS subsidiaries also requires comparable flows in the opposite direction. Here the subsidiary will need to explain to the parent the nature of its own particular developmental objectives, how they relate to established group technological norms and what precise aspects of assistance they may need from them. This 'reverse' flow then also serves a vital organisational purpose, since it will be essential for an MNE that is seeking to leverage the diverse potentials of a number of developmental subsidiaries to understand the knowledge content and specific creative aims of each. This should secure coherence in the overall programme, eliminate overlaps and redundancies in subsidiaries' exploratory agendas and aim to inculcate knowledge exchanges between subsidiaries where this seems relevant.

This latter point is depicted in Figure 7.1 by the two-way knowledge transfers between KS_3 and KS_4. Here again we accept that whilst a KS subsidiary may conceptualise a new product idea from within its own competences and define the substantive core of its creative progression around its own distinctive localised capacities and insights there may be gaps in its ability to resolve all such exploratory issues in-house. An ability and willingness to define these issues as specific questions to be addressed to sister units in the MNE then becomes a potential organisational strength in such companies. It becomes a residual centralised responsibility to inculcate an ethos of such knowledge sharing within the group and, as the most likely custodian of comprehension of 'who knows what', to bring together the most effective partners in such supportive processes. Here we can see KS_3 explaining its technology gaps and problems to KS_4 (one aspect of intra-group knowledge sharing) and receiving its help in seeking to resolve the issue. Indeed, such exploratory knowledge exchanges might lead to more substantive, less ad hoc, generation of inter-subsidiary projects, where each unit provides inputs reflecting its own localised learning potentials but builds them into complementarities with those of sister units.

Figure 7.1 also shows a second source of KS interdependencies that reflect the competitive dynamics of new product positioning within an MNE and the logical evolutionary commitments of innovation-oriented subsidiaries. Indeed, the relationship between a KS subsidiary and the future positioning of a successful product that it innovates carries persisting resonances with elements of Vernon's PLCM. The first step of this is that Figure 7.1 shows KS_3 and KS_4 as exporters, despite the fact that their host economies are likely to be relatively developed and not, therefore, innately low-cost supply bases. Several factors indicate the logic of this. Firstly, reflecting the internal logic of the innovation process itself, as propounded by Vernon, the most effective definition of the prototype production process would be in the subsidiary's host country achieved in close collaboration with the other key functions involved. Secondly, at this stage at least, the subsidiary will wish to receive the immediate rewards of being the initial producer and significant exporter of these high-value-added goods. Thirdly, the host country would expect significant benefits, not only in the high-wage rewards to the skilled and creative personnel of a KS subsidiary, but also the foreign exchange and tax revenue earned. At this stage we can see the process as having encompassed the first two stages of the traditional PLCM, with a successful innovation having promptly (but here within the decision-making scopes of a mature MNE) led to exports to other comparatively high-income economies.

But the logic of the PLCM can then continue with the relocation of the goods' production from the originating KS subsidiary to an established ES factory of the group. As illustrated in Figure 7.1, KS_3 transfers the relevant technologies to ES_2 and KS_4 to ES_1. There can be both group-level and subsidiary-level influences on this. For the MNE, once the product is fully understood and its success assured in international markets, relocation of its supply to lower-cost ES units of proven efficiency and competitiveness becomes a logical step. Here, with the firm understanding its options as a fully configured and strategically diversified network of facilities, this relocation of production does not need to wait for a major intensification of competitive supply, as was envisaged for this stage in the PLCM. The company can simply see the potential of adding cost-competitive production to the persisting benefits of the good's market-leading status. From the point of view of the subsidiary the driving motivation of its group status and its skilled personnel is not to simply prolong its supply-based rewards from post-innovation success but much more to return to its natural impulses and capacities and move towards new creative explorations.

A fundamental institutional factor conditioning this formulation of a current strategically diverse MNE is that of relatively free trade and well-honed ability of these firms to build their competitive behaviour around it. From this we have excluded a systematic role for the traditional 'tariff jumping' multi-domestic variant of MS, the defining emphasis transferring instead to the supply-side capacities of a host economy to provide viable inputs into export-oriented ES or KS roles. However, we introduce into the figure (as MS/KS_5) a more dynamic contemporary variant of MS. This, we speculate, can embed an MNE subsidiary's own distinctive competitive progression within the developmental processes of an emerging high-growth host economy. As most clearly exemplified at the moment by the case of China[17] we see the most applicable host-country context as being an already very large economy, an extremely high rate of growth and very distinctive taste patterns that are also subject to extensive change as income levels rise. In a case such as this the large size of the market and the availability of relatively low-cost inputs (access to substantial and evolving level-2 resources) can mitigate against the presumed inefficiencies of MS supply. But the challenging rates of change within the economy, its income levels and tastes, suggest that responsive supply needs to quickly go beyond adaptations of products originally developed for very different conditions.

The MS component of this revised subsidiary status reverts to an unequivocal commitment to the host-country market and allows for a supportive parent company acceptance of the degree of localised autonomy and flexible initiative required to address proactively the distinctive competitive potentials opened up there. But the complementing KS component of the positioning does add in considerable levels of complexity. Technologically, the earlier multi-domestic status of MS simply required the successful transfer of fully realised productive capabilities. Now the MS/KS variant needs to generate its own core technological competences from, in all likelihood, a range of sources.[18] The established knowledge stock of the parent company is likely, to some degree, to condition the subsidiary's creative options and choices. So the figure shows the same two-way exchanges with the parent we suggested for KS_3 and KS_4. But these established KS subsidiaries also may now be able to provide relevant technological insights, especially if they have been operating in economies with some similarities. Thus a two-way exchange is also provided with KS_4. The ability of the MS/ KS hybrid operation to put together its locally focused technologies is also likely to be constructively conditioned by inputs from the host-country's emerging science base and its informed expertise. Finally, given the decisive local-market focus of this role, the view of key inter-functional communication in the process is again emphasised. Perceptive market research, to draw out the current distinctive needs of the local market and to project their patterns into the future, is vital, as is creative engineering to secure the most efficient prototype production technologies.

As we have already observed, an important element of the heterogeneity of these MNEs was that the fundamental differences in the strategic positioning of subsidiaries required very different types of organisational practices and procedures at the group level. As expressed by Papanastassiou and Pearce (1999, 45) this range of roles that MNEs needed their subsidiaries to play meant that the emergence of heterarchy did 'not so much replace hierarchy as subsume it within heterogeneous structures and control procedures', so that 'a heterarchical MNC could easily have certain subsidiaries that were controlled in a "hierarchical" (i.e. bureaucratic) manner' (Birkinshaw and Morrison, 1995, 737). As elaborated by Birkinshaw (1994, 134) in the heterarchy lateral coordination replaces the coordination of vertical referral in a hierarchy; dispersed resources and decisions supersede centralised resources and decisions; informal control and socialisation replaces formal control mechanisms.

Applying these broad-brush principles of strategic management to our more focused concerns here we perceive the objective of an HQ as now being to secure the benefits of interdependent individualism, as the defining processes that target the coherent knowledge-based competitive development of the group. Given the exploratory uncertainties innate to the KS units it is no longer possible or desirable for HQ to seek to impose precisely defined objectives on them or to attempt any degree of interventionist control over how they pursue them. There are then two facets to what the HQ should aspire to be doing. Firstly, to understand the *individualism* that is developing in each KS operation. This should allow it to evaluate the extent and nature of each unit's potential contribution to the group's competitive enhancement and knowledge stock. But, secondly, it then needs to relate this understanding of what is emerging in each individual subsidiary to that of others, so as to determine the potentials for knowledge-exchange *interdependencies*. The HQ remains the only place in the MNE with the potential and aspiration to understand its diversified creative competences and impetus and to seek to draw them into an ever-changing and evolving, but logical and coherent, developmental group profile. As distinct from the implicit centrally determined 'master plan' of ES hierarchy, the HQ responsibility now moves to a more intuitive, perhaps improvisatory, attempt to 'juggle' and balance original KS initiatives reflecting the creative richness of diverse host locations and NSI.

NOTES

1. By contrast a key feature of level-1 primary resources, such as extracted minerals, agricultural products or forestry, was that they are completely non-renewable or only renewable 'over periods that are too long and uncertain to provide a reliable basis for sustainability' (Pearce and Zhang, 2010, 484). It was this characteristic, taken with a general desire to broaden the basis of development away from such a narrow base, that led most resource-based economies to pursue a move into industrialisation of level-2 resources. Another influence here was the persistent, if controversial, belief in a long-run deterioration in the terms of trade between primary resources and manufactured goods, provoking a movement towards capacities in the latter.
2. This clearly occupies the same strategic terrain as (Dunning, 2000) strategic asset seeking. This was defined (Dunning and Lundan, 2008, 72) as MNEs 'acquiring the assets of foreign corporations, to promote their long-term strategic objectives – especially that of sustaining or advancing their global competitiveness'. But here KS focuses more precisely on securing inputs into creative activity and extending the relevant learning processes into investigation (for example, R&D and market research) of knowledge-based potentials that have not yet been fully formulated as strategic assets.
3. In his variant of the scope typology D'Cruz (1986) describes a *branch plant* as producing for the local market. Papanastassiou and Pearce in a tripartite variant (Pearce, 1989; Papanastassiou and Pearce, 1999) depict a *truncated miniature replica*, which resembles a smaller version of the parent in terms of production and marketing responsibilities but has otherwise seriously truncated functional scope (Papanastassiou and Pearce, 1999, 24–7).
4. The first sight of such information was provided by the Report of the US Tariff Commission (1973), which presented data sourced from the US Department of Commerce. Subsequently, the Department of Commerce provided regular updates of this data in its own publications. For an overview of this early data see Pearce (1989, Tables 2.1, 2.2, 2.3).
5. Studies that used industry-level Department of Commerce data include Hirschey and Caves (1981), Lall (1979), Hewitt (1980), Pearce (1989, 60–7), Papanastassiou and Pearce (1997, 153–79) and Kumar (1996).
6. Studies that were able to use firm-level data include Mansfield et al. (1979) for US firms, Håkanson (1981) and Zejan (1990) for Swedish firms and Pearce (1989, 71–89) for firms from several national origins.
7. Papanastassiou and Pearce (1997) and Kumar (1996) tested the R&D intensity of US affiliates in different countries (R&D expenditure divided by sales) as an alternative dependent variable and found it confirmed support for local-market responsiveness as a positive determinant of R&D decentralisation. Using survey data from 1978 for Swedish MNE subsidiaries, Zejan (1990) found GDP to be consistently significantly positively related to their R&D intensity, whether these subsidiaries focused on adaptation or developmental activity.
8. The difficulty of deriving adequate proxies for the minimum efficient scale of R&D operations meant that rigorous testing of these perspectives proved rare and indecisive. Hirschey and Caves (1981, 118–19) found their proxy to indeed be a significant negative determinant of overseas R&D. Hewitt (1980, 320) found two alternative estimates of

R&D economies of scale to be insignificant as determinants, though this was actually in line with his 'agnostic' predictions for the relationship.

9. In the same way if a high level of use of a central laboratory was considered necessary to fully employ outstanding specialists based there in the work at which they excel, this may become less relevant if they can spend some time visiting and supporting development projects in decentralised units (Pearce, 1989, 39).

10. In fact, Papanastassiou and Pearce (1997) used the 'share of US subsidiaries' production in a country which is supplied to the local (that is, host-country) market'. But we can here interpret this as the export-orientation variable.

11. In his tests for Swedish firms Zejan (1990) found that positive relationship to be confirmed for both adaptation and product-development-oriented R&D units. The result for product development is compatible with PM-type behaviour. For adaptation he argues (Zejan, 1990, 491) it may involve 'the adaptation of products to regional conditions', suggesting a constrained regional location decision that still leaves room for some process adaptation.

12. Ronstadt's interviews found that overseas production and marketing managers favoured the setting up of TTUs when they felt that product and process technologies were still unsettled, so that there could be a stream of technical service projects to assimilate it locally. Thus TTUs might operate to support the prompt application by overseas subsidiaries of products that were still in an evolving stage of the innovation process, so that they could help put the 'finishing touches' to the formulation of the product (with particular reference to their own market). This would reflect our argument in Chapter 3 that once a firm had become an MNE the demand of ambitious subsidiaries for access to new centrally created innovations could, in effect, collapse the first two stages of Vernon's PLCM into one dispersed process.

13. In the terms we adopt here we can see Behrman and Fischer's world-market MNEs as being, perhaps, an evolving hybrid of the network hierarchy and the heterarchy.

14. It should indeed be noted that since Behrman and Fischer categorised each firm by its currently dominant strategic orientation, the limited numbers of fully formulated world-market MNEs does not preclude an extensive emerging presence for such commitments. This would be a logical progression for host-market MNEs in particular.

15. The roots of this remain firmly in the work of Ronstadt but as refocused by Haug et al. (1983) and Hood and Young (1982) and adapted and applied by Pearce (1989, 1999), Pearce and Papanastassiou (1999) and Papanastassiou and Pearce (1999, 149–59).

16. Papanastassiou and Pearce (1999, 151–5) indicate an alternative positioning of support laboratory responsibilities (designated as SL2). Here the part of the group (parent company or subsidiary) that has a full comprehension of the technology to be transferred (which they will have created themselves or have previously assimilated and operationalised) will undertake responsibility. They will thus organise an 'outward' transfer of the technology or assist (in a 'tutor' role) the recipient subsidiary in learning, assimilating and, as appropriate, adapting it.

17. The range of roles played by MNE subsidiaries in China, and their processes of evolution within China's development, are reviewed by Zhang and Pearce (2012, 43–71).

18. The diverse sources of technology available to MNE subsidiaries in China were analysed by Zhang and Pearce (2012, 73–99).

8. Multinationals from emerging economies: a new challenge of practice to theory

So far a central theme of our understanding of the development of IB has been the ways in which MNEs were able to adjust their competitive bases and organisational structures in response to changes in the international economic environment. A major component of this, we argued, was the intensification of global competition due to the emergence of many new MNEs, with the rise of important new source countries distinguished as a crucial factor in this. An assumption behind the latter point, however, was that the appearance of MNEs from a new source country was a natural process embedded organically in that country's development. MNEs would only arise *once* their home country had achieved levels of industrial and institutional maturity that allowed the firms to determine and trust their viability as international operations. It was a firm-level decision but one decisively conditioned by strengths of the home-country economy.

But these historically based *theoretical* perspectives cannot approach provision of an explanation for perhaps the most challenging and idiosyncratic phenomena in recent IB *practice*: the appearance of significant MNEs from emerging economies such as China and India. This has provoked a very earnest debate as to whether or not we need a 'new theory' to explain these emerging economy MNEs (EE-MNEs) (Narula, 2006, 2012). Here we will argue that, in the end, we do not. The broad theoretical perspectives reviewed in the earlier chapters can ultimately provide effective bases for development of an understanding of the EE-MNEs. We will suggest it does this in two ways. Firstly, the extant theories still provide a good foundation for the articulation of what *is*, indeed, idiosyncratic about these enterprises. Secondly, with this comprehension in place, it is through the adaptation and refocusing of elements of the theoretical constructs that we can provide a framework to analyse the challenging characteristics and developmental positioning of the EE-MNEs. In fact, rather more in line with the first paragraph above, we can suggest that the key conditioning difference between 'traditional' MNEs and 'new' EE-MNEs lies in their external contexts; the status of the *national* economy from which they emerge and the *international* economy they seek to enter. In effect the paradox of EE-MNEs is that they can emerge very *early* in the development of their domestic economy but very *late* in the formulation of the international economy they seek to enter.

Building on these perspectives it has proved useful (Tang, 2014; Tang and Pearce, 2011, 2014, 2017) to begin the process of constructing a *theoretical* approach to EE-MNEs by drawing out precise aspects of the ways they appear to differ from traditional 'Western' MNEs, and to find their *practice* embedded in the needs of a distinctively different context; that of home-country development. We can start this analytical process by indicating three particular characteristics of the way in which the new EE-MNEs appear to defy expectations innate to the traditional mainstream theorising, and then draw from each of them pointers towards particular facets of a repositioned theorising. The core of this refocusing, we will suggest, will be to combine persisting *micro*-level characterisations of these EE-MNEs with a more challenging comprehension of their distinctive positioning within the *macro*-level development of their home economies.

The central presumption of how the now mainstream IB theorising interpreted the emergence of the traditional post-war generation of pioneering MNEs was that these firms' entry into overseas production occurred when they, of their own volition and discretion, felt that they had the capacity to do this and could discern precise reasons and opportunities for doing so. Two further assumptions can be seen to have underpinned this characterisation. Firstly, that those firms would have only been able to generate such strong and distinctive sources of international competitiveness over quite extended periods of time, during which their own development would have been integral to the gradualist processes of industrial and technological progression of their home country. Secondly, this would imply that such pioneering MNEs would only have emerged from a select group of high-income, technologically experienced, economies whose mature and quite stabilised industrial sectors operated independently from any degree of significant day-to-day government interventions.

Two of the central tenets of the demand for, at least, a reformulated approach to theorising on EE-MNEs reflect, very precisely, the seeming redundancy of these two presumptions ingrained in modelling the traditional MNEs. Firstly, it is accepted that EE-MNEs commence their international expansion long before their home countries have reached the level of industrial maturity or technological strength that the traditional theorising would have considered to be necessary. Secondly, in the light of this presumption, these firms could not yet have completed the in-house formulation of their own unique and distinctive sources of competitive advantage (OAs) to a level that could provide the basis for their confidant and discretionary choice of international expansion. Both of these contentions will feed into a repositioning of aspects of established IB thinking to provide a basis for understanding EE-MNEs. In particular we will argue that the basic concept of OA remains relevant to analysis of EE-MNEs but in a rather different contextualisation and with an alternative interpretation of its relevant competitive 'relativity'.

The second implicit assumption we find in the traditional IB theorising again points towards the need to see the positioning of the emergence of EE-MNEs as a reflection of a very different home-country situation. Here the early theory's central emphasis on the initial expansion of MNEs as an essentially micro firm-level decision choice precluded any systematic role for home-country governments. The firms believed they possessed the competitive abilities that would allow for the initiation of successful international operations and were themselves able to perceive, in the light of their own comprehension of their precise strengths, where such opportunities existed in foreign economies. Such decisions were thus assumed to be made and implemented independently, with no expectation of support from their government or as, in any way, a response to its policies or wishes.[1] Though we find the ability of these MNEs to expand into foreign operations to reflect the level of development achieved by their domestic economy there was no sense in which such firm-level internationalisation was perceived (by firms or governments) as playing a role in the furtherance of this development. Theorising on EE-MNEs precisely resiles from such perspectives. As we will develop here, those firms do *need* various forms of government support and *receive* it because of their capacity to achieve certain policy objectives that do reflect the country's state of development. The *micro* expansion of EE-MNEs is now endogenous to, and contextualised by, the *macro* concerns of their home-country development.

The third presumption that we can now see as implicit in the dominant modes of analysis of the traditional MNEs' internationalisation was that, in terms developed later, the strategic motivation was that of the improved *exploitation* of their firm-specific sources of competitive advantage. In short-term perspectives the firms are satisfied with their established sources of competitiveness but perceive ways in which their rewards from them can be enhanced by moving them into operations based in foreign locations. The first of these was that of market seeking (MS) in which the MNEs extended their production into an overseas economy as the best means of securing, under prevailing conditions (for example, high levels of trade restraint), optimal returns from their competitive advantages. In the theorising we have seen this scenario as the motivation leading to overseas production in the second stage of Vernon's PLCM and also as the basis for the 'trade-destroying FDI' that Kojima diagnosed as prevailing in the early post-war decades. Subsequently, efficiency seeking (ES), as cost-effective production in an overseas location for export markets, emerged as an alternative means of improving exploitation of existing firm-specific competitiveness. Again Vernon's PLCM predicted this in its standardised product stage and Kojima advocated it as the source of 'trade-creating FDI'.

But, as already emphasised, MS and ES as motivations for overseas expansion were predicated on the firms' possession (or belief that they possessed) international quality OAs through which they could assert and optimise their position in global markets. The key assumption (the first point above) of current thinking on EE-MNE is that they *do not* yet possess OAs of this quality. Therefore, it is not expected that MS or ES will provide the initiating motivation for EE-MNE expansion. For similar reasons we have also asserted that the EE-MNE are unlikely to internationalise purely of their own volition, so that when they do so it becomes dependent on support from their home government and because it is considered that they can play roles in securing benefits relating to the wider developmental needs of the economy. The framework we will adopt here can emphasise (especially in reflection of the China case) two particular roles for such FDI; resource seeking (RS) and knowledge seeking (KS).[2]

To show how these challenges to traditional theorising can be effectively addressed through the refocusing of its basic concepts and analytical perspectives we can adopt a four-part framework (Tang and Pearce, 2014, 2017) for understanding the nature and positioning of EE-MNEs, derived initially to elaborate the case of Chinese MNEs. There are two central themes in the framework, developing points made earlier. Firstly, it will adopt a conventional view of OAs (rebranded as FSA-A) as the defining feature of the firm's competitive progression to internationalisation; but as operationalised in a very different context in terms of where and how the advantage is manifest and exercised. Secondly, the key facet of this repositioning of the firm's contextualisation places it within the discretion and priorities of the home-country government and its policies towards the sustainability of national development.

The adoption of the *conventional* traditional OA_a, designated in the framework as *asset* firm-specific advantage (FSA-A) (Tang and Pearce, 2017), faces two analytical challenges in terms of an *unconventional* position in an exploration of the EE-MNE. Firstly, the expectation that an EE-MNE will not have achieved FSA-A of such competitive maturity that it can leverage them as the core of an independently chosen entry into international operations. Secondly, that the FSA-A's initial international application will be mediated through the pursuit of a role within its home-country development programmes. These two perspectives have been brought together in the familiar strand of analysis in EE-MNEs that has asserted that such firms internationalise because their in-house limitations are alleviated and augmented by various sources of government support. To provide the context, it is useful to anticipate subsequent detail by suggesting that high-growth emerging economies are likely to find the sustainability and renewal of their prevailing modes of development compromised by emerging resource shortages and knowledge constraints. Often the most immediately available means of alleviating such imbalances appears to be overseas sourcing, with FDI accepted as the most viable means of achieving it. From this perspective macro policy then devolves particular strategic objectives (we have pointed to RS and KS in the Chinese case) onto potential MNEs.

This takes us back to the micro context of MNE expansion; *which* MNEs emerge to play these roles mandated by macro factors? It is here that the framework asserts the revised 'relativity' for the role of OAs; it should be the firm with the strongest and most appropriate FSA-A that emerges to undertake the necessary act of FDI and acquire the home-country supports to do so. Their 'advantage' is relative to other home-country enterprises that might aspire to the same FDI opportunity. This points again to the much-revised nature of the FDI decision process. In traditional MNEs we have seen this to be a purely 'commercial' process in which the firm, entirely through its own information and judgement, decides that the most effective further exploitation of its sources of competitiveness require entry into overseas operations. The ability to make and implement this choice merely requires the further extension of its established managerial practices. The sources of mature competitiveness lead *directly* to FDI. By contrast EE-MNEs can expect to leverage their FSA-A as the basis for internationalisation, but only through an *indirect* route through the bureaucratic procedures and institutional policies and practices of the home-country government and the perceived needs of its developmental objectives. In acceptance of this the framework argues that a firm aspiring to become an EE-MNE will need a very different type of managerial expertise, the ability to understand these governmental decision-making institutions and procedures and to operate effectively within them. This is described as *relationship* firm-specific advantage (FSA-R) with its broad objective being to project the strength and appropriateness of the firm's FSA-A as the basis for implementing aspects of the government's development-oriented international policies.[3]

As argued by Tang and Pearce (2017) from the Chinese case, the development of FSA-R may be a natural element within the early formulation of such firms in a way that would not have been necessary in the traditional MNEs. Chinese firms, for example, will have emerged not only during periods of very high levels of *economic* growth and competitive change but also during times when defining elements of the *institutional* environment will have been initially formulated and then subject to frequent revision. In this environment it will have been an essential aspect of their constitution and formation as firms to learn 'to understand, tolerate and derive flexibility as a response to, such institutional volatility and endemic change'. This inculcates, as a natural capacity, the FSA-R that provide the aspirant EE-MNE with the ability to build up and nurture relationships with the developmental institutions and agencies that may define those FDI opportunities towards which it can 'spin' the relevance of its FSA-A. Indeed, these types of relationship building capacities may be relevant to not only securing participation in an FDI project but also to its effective execution where this may involve negotiations and sustained interactions with *host-country* institutions.

These modes of thinking do, of course, have some provenance in wider analyses in IB. Thus Peng et al. (2005, 623–4) presented institutional relatedness 'as the degree of informal embeddedness or interconnectedness with dominant institutions [which] confers resources and increases the legitimacy of an organisation' in ways that build ties within 'a dense network . . . of dominant institutions'. Also the conceptualisation of institutional ownership advantages (Dunning and Lundan, 2008; Lundan, 2010) discussed here in Chapter 2 has clear resonances with FSA-R, as did Dunning's (2002) earlier articulation of firm-specific relational assets as 'the stock of a firm's willingness and capability to access, shape and engage in economically beneficial relationships; and to sustain and upgrade those relationships'.

Moving explicitly into the case of Chinese MNEs Buckley et al. (2007, 502) suggest these firms may have 'special ownership advantages' in terms of 'the ability to engage in beneficial relations with firms and other actors to provide access to resources controlled by others'. Similarly, Buckley et al. (2011, 135–6) argue that where an economic system is built around 'relations-based' governance systems this 'may reward personal linkages between business and government', whilst Rugman (2010, 84) suggests that 'MNEs from emerging markets [need] to develop FSA in business-government relations'. Finally, in an analysis of the determinants of Chinese FDI, Wang et al. (2012, 672) indicate that firm-level resource (that is, FSA-A) only leads to internationalisation of operations 'when firms are strongly supported by government' so that an EE-MNE's 'ability to employ its resources and internationalise depends on its effectiveness in managing government ties' (that is, FSA-R).[4]

The idea of country-specific advantage (CSA) has long been accepted as a defining element in a very influential mode of IB theorising (Rugman, 1981; Rugman and Verbeke, 2009; Rugman et al., 2011). As such its role has been to delineate the range of country (host and/or home)-level factors that determine the participation and purpose of MNEs. The derivation of a refocused version of CSA in the framework for analysis of EE-MNEs that is adopted here underlines an important subtext of this chapter; that new phenomena in IB can be most effectively comprehended through adapted tenets of proven methodologies. Here two variants of CSA are derived to place the practical emergence of EE-MNEs within the economic and institutional formulation of their home countries. Firstly, *developmental* country-specific advantages (CSA-D) formalises the themes of EE-MNEs' mandated participation in response to the dynamic forces and imbalances of the country's high growth. Secondly, *institutional* country-specific advantages (CSA-I) seek to show how particular policies and institutions of the home country can indeed determine *which* firms become EE-MNEs and *what* benefits they are expected to obtain through their supported FDI.

To elaborate these home-country perspectives we project CSA-D as a range of influences endogenous to the country's development that can provide sources of support to its potential EE-MNEs but also generate the need for such FDI and thereby determine the motivations to be pursued through the firms' roles in it.[5] Of course any successful process of economic growth should generate re-investable resources and ought to logically define roles for this within its evolutionary sustainability. But the position we see for CSA-D in the development of current high-growth emerging economies is much more structurally strategic, indicating crucial roles for FDI and EE-MNEs in addressing imbalances and securing renewed bases for the perpetuation of this progress. As noted earlier in this chapter, and in line with the longer-term theories of this narrative, important practical features of CSA-D reflect a crucial factor in the performance of these economies and the early emergence of their MNEs. They benefit from, but are also challenged by, immediate participation in a much more open, diverse and competitive *international* economy.

It is a central tenet in standard growth theory that the generation of a capital surplus routinely results in reinvestment in the domestic economy as the logical means of sustaining that performance. It is also assumed in this scenario that this process of investment occurs through a capital market that discerns the most plausible growth opportunities. The much more pervasive acceptance of the international context for the achievements of the high-growth emerging economies changes these perspectives. Once again their growth does generate an important capital surplus but – seeing this as now an element in the positive aspects of CSA-D – positions it in a much more institutional and policy-based developmental context that places it as a means of support for FDI as an integral component in addressing constraints and imbalances in growth. As notably exemplified in the Chinese case capital surpluses can be co-opted by financial institutions beyond the market and *allocated* to support EE-MNEs.

As has again been most visibly and powerfully exemplified by the case of China, a frequent manifestation of high rates of growth has been the running of persistent balance of payments surpluses and, therefore, the generation of very large foreign exchange reserves. This then also becomes a significant aspect of CSA-D since it is possible to control access to such reserves so that they can be applied in support of specific acts of FDI and to the expansion of particular EE-MNEs. As with capital, foreign exchange becomes an initially macro-level resource reflective of ongoing development that can be leveraged to enable EE-MNEs to secure participation in investment opportunities that meet home-country needs but which their FSA-A could not access on their own.

An important common situation facing the recent generation of emerging-market economies has been the need to assert their competitiveness in the intense trade conditions of a very open global economy. A range of institutional arrangements has emerged that broadly seeks to condition the environment in ways that can help this. These arrangements can include well-motivated commercial departments in embassies and consulates; distribution and information exchange arrangements with local enterprises in target markets; government supported participation in trade fairs and similar PR opportunities. The main purposes of such practices and agencies have been to improve the situation for trade in important host countries. But with the increasing relevance of FDI such associations and arrangements can also provide knowledge and experience that is conducive to logical FDI decisions and supportive of their effective execution. In this way these agencies of international economic policies can be seen as another positive element in CSA-D, emerging in the home economy's early trade-based growth but increasingly supportive of its continuation through carefully formulated FDI.

These factors represent the positive face of CSA-D, since they show how manifestations of the success of development can support the *ability* of EE-MNEs to carry out acts of FDI where these are considered to be necessary. Against this, the negative face of CSA-D represents specific forces that reflect endemic problems of sustainability and regeneration in the high-growth developing economies and that, therefore, provide *motivations* for FDI as an approach to their alleviation. If positive CSA-D can help explain *how* EE-MNEs can emerge, the negative ones help define *why* they do so. Building on the Chinese case (Tang and Pearce, 2017) we analyse two motivations for its FDI that can be interpreted as responses to vulnerabilities in the sustainability of its development processes. These reflect two different phases and issues in sustainability. The first, RS, can be projected as a means of prolonging the viability of its current modes of development, whilst the second, KS, attempts to generate means of extending it into new upgraded possibilities.

It has become a familiar 'stylised fact' that primary-resource shortages have emerged as a significant brake on China's current dominant mode of industrialisation and development and that, therefore, this has led to a major programme of international sourcing (Moyo, 2012). This may reflect a quite general developmental tendency such that 'where early-stage growth is decisively based around a dominant resource (such as labour) the planning processes may somewhat neglect the significance of relevant secondary resources (such as energy or minerals) until constraining shortages begin to emerge' (Tang and Pearce, 2017). In the terms introduced in Chapter 7 the assumption has been that the core of Chinese growth was decisively focused on the exploitation of level-2 resources, in terms of a highly efficient supply of productive labour underpinning a cost-competitive export-oriented industrialisation. As such this was considered to be sustainable in both quantitative and qualitative terms. Thus, until relatively recently, the supply of such labour was believed to be quite elastic, whilst the capacity for upgrading its productive potentials, through higher skill levels, could feed into continuation of higher-value-added output. The more immediately challenging imbalance was, therefore, seen to be an inability of local sources of level-1 inputs (for example, energy and minerals) to keep up with demand driven by the core processes. Developmental policy, here reflecting a negative aspect of CSA-D, needed to address this through external sourcing, building a major role for RS operations in China's new MNEs.[6]

This modelling of the resource restructuring within China's evolving development can also provide us with the roots of our second facet of negative CSA-D; that is, KS. We have just seen how the prolongation of the pioneering export-oriented cost-competitive industrialisation could be addressed by the persistent upgrading of level-2 resources in the form of labour productivity. But as we saw in Chapter 7 it is not part of the scope of level-2 resources to provide the higher-value-added production processes that allow for their upgraded application. This requires the presence of the creative level-3 resources to achieve the innovations that facilitate enhanced performance from level-2 inputs. It becomes a developmental priority to address KS as a key imperative in sustainability, creating, accessing and providing new scopes to industry. In China this has led to a strong commitment to an NSI to source these new potentials. But, as argued in Chapter 7, the range of new global knowledge sources (technological and market heterogeneity) has led to an acceptance that, however strong a country's own commitment to KS, and however effectively its firms can feed off this, both (the country and its business) need to approach KS on an international basis. This has resulted in KS being a motivation for China's MNEs that has become central to this facet of its international developmental strategies. In effect the support for firm-level KS FDI becomes integral to the imperatives pursued in the domestic NSI.

It is useful to elaborate a little on this positioning for KS in EE-MNEs. Firstly, because it can exemplify the distinctive ways in which the early internationalisation of these firms reflects processes that are integral to both their formulation as firms and the competitive development of their home economy. Secondly, because elaborating this within a particular EE-MNE-focused analytical framework can show how understanding this new phenomenon can elaborate effectively on, rather than undermine, our established modes of thinking in IB. In this respect we can draw in the firm-level positioning of FSA-A at the core of both the theorising of KS and its practical execution.

In our exposition of KS in traditional MNEs in the previous chapter we saw this as a logically evolutionary process that sought to add new sources of competitiveness to what were already considered to be (in our current terms) a mature and proven body of successful FSA-A. We can now see that this routinely path-dependent learning process provided two roles for these established FSA-A. They would serve to clarify the types of new knowledge to be sought, intending this to ideally add coherently to current sources of competitiveness, without unduly undermining or destabilising these established norms. Also, the ability to explore, assess and, if relevant, co-opt and coherently draw in such KS possibilities is likely to be carried out by those personnel with the fullest understanding of the current FSA-A and its strengths and limitations.

Our view of KS in Chinese and other EE-MNEs indicates a very different and more analytically challenging perspective. For these 'new' MNEs the role of KS is 'not to add incrementally to fully formulated and successful FSA-A, but to acquire externally knowledge-based inputs' that can fuel the learning 'processes that are attempting to achieve the sorts of unique and distinctive FSA-A that [could eventually] define genuine international competitiveness for the Chinese MNEs' (Tang and Pearce, 2017). These are projected here as exploratory 'gap-filling' objectives, by contrast to the logically informed and evolutionary ones of KS for the traditional MNEs.

But this takes us back to the central enigma of EE-MNEs. It accepts that the KS investments are being made precisely because the EE-MNEs understand the limitations of their current FSA-A. But mainstream theorising has always asserted that successful FDI needs a strong basis in fully formulated sources of international competitiveness, that is, mature FSA. Against this theorising how can EE-MNEs undertake KS FDI that is precisely motivated to overcome perceived limitations in their FSA-A? As we have seen, the EE-MNE framework resolves the firm-level conundrum by repositioning it in the macro-level dynamics of the home-country development, a response to a clearly understood aspect of negative CSA-D. The firm discusses (in an application of FSA-R) possible participation in a KS project, advocating its relevance to the country's knowledge-based development and the firm's own capacity (relative to other *local* firms) to execute it effectively. If successful, the firm expects the types of positive CSA-D supports that the framework advocates.

There is another aspect of the different positioning of KS in traditional MNEs and EE-MNEs that points towards the logic and necessity of government support in the latter case. This accepts that KS is, by definition, an exploratory process the value of whose outcome is, therefore, uncertain. But the expectation for the traditional MNEs is that, because they hope to build in a logically informed and evolutionary manner on fully defined existing FSA-A, they should be able to locate and execute KS decisions with a reasonably high level of realistic potential. But our characterisation of EE-MNEs' KS decisions is very different. They are much more intuitively exploratory, seeking to fill gaps in their current knowledge competences that they are often not yet able to fully articulate. Whereas this may open up the serendipitous discovery of much more radical breakthrough potentials, it also risks a large number of poor under-informed KS decisions that achieve little of relevance. Exploring these unknown KS potentials as a source of the types of desirable new level-3 resources may be more amenable to government decision makers than the more constrained scopes of the putative MNEs that are nevertheless considered the most logical vehicle to pursue them. This again points to government support for the KS roles of, for example, Chinese MNEs.

The practicalities of securing these developmental interdependencies between EE-MNEs and their home economies need to be realised within the operations of specific institutions. Therefore, the framework is completed by formalising CSA-I, encompassing the range of arrangements and institutions that firms seeking to expand internationally will need to negotiate with and operate within so as to secure access to the support they need to activate and supplement their FSA-A.[7] It is, thus, the defining context for the application of their FSA-R. The precise forms taken by these institutions will, inevitably, vary between countries and also evolve through time in each one. Our focus here, therefore, will not be on such specific practical formulations but rather address the notable ways conceptualising CSA-I adds to theorising.

Buckley et al. (2011, 125–6) build on North's (1990) classic exposition to indicate that institutions 'coordinate aspects of the domestic economy, are partially codified and contain an element of enforcement and sanction'. Therefore they can encompass both formal elements, such as the country's 'legislature, judiciary and bureaucracy, government structures and market mechanisms', and more informal elements such as social networks. In terms of the institutional context addressed by aspirant EE-MNEs from economies such as China it is the *way* that relevant domestic markets work or become subject to distortions or failures that is relevant. Here we can look for any discriminatory preferences, and similar imperfections that can make particular factors and influences more readily available to the firms that wish, or are to be encouraged, to exploit them as a basis for particular overseas investment projects.[8]

In line with this Buckley et al. (2011, 136) note that 'close relationships and collusion between government and domestic businesses can lead to structures and endemic market imperfections which are exploitable by companies that enjoy good relationships with the administration'. Similarly, Voss (2011, 91–2) argues that China's outward FDI 'regime has been characterised by market imperfections that arise from the need of firms to be well aligned with government officials and the status and economic rank of companies'. From this 'relational access to government bodies that can grant necessary approvals remain an important asset to companies' (Voss, 2011, 90), that is, our FSA-R.

Luo et al. (2010, 68) address similar concepts by indicating the need to closely examine 'the regulatory pillar of the home country's institutional environment, particularly specific policies enacted by home-country governments' in order to fully comprehend how such governments can nurture the growth of their emerging MNEs through the promoting of relevant acts of FDI.[9] They also observe (2010, 69) how 'the Chinese government specifically promotes outward foreign direct investment (OFDI) for the interest of national economic development' alongside its support for individual firms, placing the institutional (CSA-I) at the disposal of the developmental (CSA-D) concerns. In addition, echoing FSA-R, Luo et al. (2010, 78) argue that for emerging economy enterprises to access the benefits of these forms of government support 'they need to familiarise with government policies, consistently communicate with government agencies, join government-specialised institutions, and actively influence new policies and measures'.

We can conclude by showing how these themes operate in one practical context, access to capital. Here Voss (2011, 5) argues very pertinently that the ability of Chinese firms to pursue international opportunities 'may not necessarily mean managerial capacity and technological advancement over competitors, but access to financial resources'. Thus 'the possibility to internalise access to abundant funding may help Chinese firms to overcome competitive weaknesses and invest abroad' so as to 'pursue aims beyond immediate firm-level profitability'. These lines of argument underline two vital analytical perspectives. Firstly, that the ability to leverage capital market imperfections is a source of exploitable advantage for potential EE-MNEs (Buckley, 2004; Buckley et al., 2007, 2011). Secondly, that their ability to secure this capital in an institutional (rather than pure-market) context may reflect a willingness and capacity to work within wider programmes of home-government policy instead of the immediate pursuit of conventional profit-seeking motivations.

The framework presented here invokes a range of areas of established theorising in order to define the diverse influences that are operating as determinants in the *emergence* of the path-breaking new generation of EE-MNEs. We can see that the follow-up challenge in the practical analysis of these firms is then to understand their *evolution* as MNEs. To what extent, and how quickly, might such firms begin to escape from roots in home-country policies and to assert a degree of independence as enterprises with fully formulated globally competitive horizons? To reassert a very traditional IB perspective the key question may then become how quickly can such new MNEs reach genuine global standards of competitiveness (that is, fully developed FSA-A), and will being already internationally operative have helped or hindered progress towards this status?

We can in fact discern the nature of these evolutionary possibilities from within the analytical structures previously outlined to track the origins of the EE-MNEs. The central enigma there, we saw, was that these firms were enabled to expand internationally despite limited FSA-A capabilities that, in turn, reflected relatively low levels of home-country technological and competitive development. The corollary of this is that upon internationalisation an EE-MNE finds itself in an environment that, whilst obviously very challenging, also provides it with extensive new learning potentials. It does find itself in a competitive situation where the limitations of its current FSA-A are going to be clearly exposed, but also one where it now has more informed access to the current norms and the potential to learn from them and move its capacities towards them.[10] This, our framework tells us, will be conditional on home-country support persisting long enough for these potentials to be realised and, indeed, for home-country policymakers to be amenable to these firms evolving in ways that are likely to move their strongest competitive bases and operative contexts away from their domestic roots. Given such an acceptance then, the new challenge to practical research agendas will be to understand the potential metamorphosis of Chinese and other EE-MNEs into fully formulated and independently motivated globally focused enterprises. Again our extant theorising can provide some suggestions in articulating this agenda.

The first step in this is to reassert the importance of the relative strength and distinctive characteristics of the FSA-A that did underpin the firm's initial overseas operations. It should be from a thorough understanding of these domestically derived initial attributes that the internationalising firm can formulate a carefully informed evaluation of their specific limitations when confronted by international norms. Similarly, as our previous discussion of KS has indicated, it can only be from an informed basis in existing FSA-A that the firm can execute effective learning processes; by detecting potential sources of new capacities, accessing them and building them into upgraded competitive capacities. An immediate implication of this interpretation of the learning processes in the EE-MNEs is that, for all their perceived limitations, it is their home-country FSA-A that conditions the way their competitiveness is upgraded internationally; their initial progress is evolutionary and still with home-country roots.

Then a very interesting question will be whether this will persist into the longer term? Will MNEs with Chinese and other emerging economy origins retain distinctive home-country characteristics in perpetuity and, if so, what might these be? Or will their internationalised context come to prevail with a more diversified set of competences and characteristics focused in a more neutral way on global competitiveness? This longer-term perspective on the evolution of these firms *as* MNEs then points to a separate, equally vital, learning context. If their growth comes to embrace the aspects of geographical and strategic diversity expected of a fully mature MNE this will require organisational and managerial competences very different from those that would have prevailed during their home-country origination and their first international expansions. Once again these new MNEs will have the scope to learn these norms quite quickly from operating in a competitive environment that is determined by the behaviour of the firms that will have established these practices and procedures over longer periods of time. Ultimately, the success of these evolving EE-MNEs will depend on their ability to exercise the 'latecomer' learning potentials sufficiently to overcome the innate liabilities of 'foreignness' and 'newness'.

NOTES

1. The main emphasis of policies in these areas took the form of macro-level capital controls to limit OFDI. In fact, as carefully argued by Buckley et al. (2010), the articulation of these controls tended to derive from neoclassical frameworks and neglected the micro-level comprehension of MNEs and their behaviour that was appearing from IB analysis.
2. Pioneering 1985 Chinese documentation setting out principles for OFDI approval procedures established four categories of projects likely to be acceptable. Firstly, those aimed at securing international access to domestically scarce natural resources (that is, RS). Secondly, those capable of acquiring technology and transferring it back to China (that is, KS). Thirdly, projects that could increase managerial skills through 'on-the-job' training; another learning process reflecting KS objectives. Fourthly, projects enhancing the export potentials available to Chinese companies; a variant of MS. In theoretical terms it is worth noting that none of these early government-supported FDI motivations are oriented towards the exploitation of mature firm-level capabilities (OA/FSA) in the way expected of the traditional MNEs.
3. Tang and Pearce (2017) define FSA-R as 'a firm's managerial abilities to establish, nurture and draw benefits from external relationships, through which they seek to secure preferred access to what are, at least initially, generally available sources of support'.
4. There are potentially significant *normative* (or evaluative) issues relating to how the relationship between FSA-A and FSA-R might affect the efficiency of realisation of the true performance potentials of an investment project that an EE-MNE might become part of. This is relevant to host economies, affecting how well they might secure the developmental potential of a resource base (RS investment) or achieve the most valuable realisation of the creative scopes in its knowledge base (KS investment). Here a positive *complementary* relationship would prevail if a very strong FSA-R made sure that a project was implemented by the EE-MNE with the ideal FSA-A so as to fully realise its best potentials. By contrast, a negative result would occur if very persuasive FSA-R led to a project being executed by far from ideal FSA-A (excluding better available ones). Similarly, the best available FSA-A might not be selected if the potential investor's FSA-R failed to project the case persuasively.
5. Tang and Pearce (2017) define CSA-D as 'forces that are endogenous to a country's developmental processes that generate resources and/or motivations that can drive and support the international expansion of its firms'.
6. In response to these perceptions most of the studies of the determinants of China's FDI included variables attempting to assess the presence of the RS motivation. Though there have been, perhaps inevitably, some ambiguities in these studies two results seem to have come into focus. Firstly, as indicated by Buckley et al. (2007, 511) 'that the securement of natural resources has become an imperative in more recent years, in line with Chinese domestic growth'. Secondly, RS commitments become more focused on developing countries, with Africa emerging as a very significant location. This may confirm that government support for RS FDI may play wider roles in important aspects of China's economic and diplomatic foreign policies.
7. Tang and Pearce (2017) define CSA-I as 'those facets of a country's institutional environment that determine and guide the motivations for an MNE to address particular overseas investment projects and/or provide it with the scope to leverage discriminatory access to resources that help facilitate such acts of internationalisation'.
8. Studies that provide valuable and interpretative detail on how CSA-I have evolved within China's development include Luo et al. (2010, 72–5), Buckley et al. (2007, 504), Cross et al. (2007, 61) and Voss (2011, 66–92).
9. In an analysis of the determinants of new overseas investments in particular countries by Chinese firms from 2002/09 Lu et al. (2014) show that 'home country support' policy is a consistently positive influence, for both developed and developing host countries. The study also shows that the *more* important is this government support in the case of a

particular investment the *less* relevant would be experience of the host country through earlier investment. If such prior entries can be seen to have possibly served to alleviate liability of foreignness, then the results of Lu et al. suggest that elements of government support provide an alternative means of achieving this. Thus if CSA-D point to a desirable entry into a foreign location then aspects of CSA-I support can help to facilitate this, even if the potential investing firm does not itself have previous experience of the country.

10. The 'leverage', 'linking' and 'learning' approach of Mathews (2002, 2006a, 2006b) provides insights along these lines.

9. Evaluating the multinational: a coda

INTRODUCTION

An essential background to this narrative has been that the growth of international *business* has been integral to the growth of an international *economy* that has itself been an increasingly pervasive determinant of the performance of individual *national* economies. From this the academic discipline of IB derived its core mandate, to *understand* the MNE as a key agent driving this economic globalisation. Building on a careful and thorough analysis of the practicalities of the expansion of MNEs, the theorising generated in IB then addressed the central questions of 'how' such firms could emerge, 'why' and 'when' they did so and 'where' they chose to operate. The earlier chapters have elaborated a number of analytical frameworks that have aimed to provide us with the means to understand the reality of such participation in the wider global economy. Here we seek to conclude by approaching this knowledge from a rather different direction in order to address another, perhaps somewhat neglected, concern; to *evaluate* the behaviour and performance of MNEs in terms of normative criteria derived mainly from beyond the innate interests of mainstream IB analysis and practice.

Here we can adopt and develop an 'evaluation framework' (Dunning and Pearce, 1994; Pearce, 2006) that aims to distinguish between four different generic issues relating to the performance and implications of MNEs' participation in a global economy that is comprised of separately motivated and competitively distinctive national economies, namely 'efficiency', 'distribution (or fairness)', 'sovereignty' and 'growth and development'. Seeking to delineate the elements of each of these issues implies two key subtexts derived from our earlier analysis. Firstly, at the practical level, we can trace changes in the normative performance implications of MNEs as they adjusted the parameters of their competitive behaviour in response to changes in the international economy in which they were operating. Did the realities of globalisation affect the contributions of MNE operations in ways that wider normative concerns could consider to be positive or negative? Secondly, at the more theoretical level, what are the implications of the pervasive association of MNEs with various types of market imperfections? Are key elements of MNEs' behaviour and, therefore, performance mainly determined by their ability to feed off, exploit and perhaps even enhance or generate, inefficiencies in relevant markets? Or do the ways they operate in unavoidably imperfect markets offset the inefficiencies of these markets, reduce the costs of their use and, ultimately, improve performance?

EFFICIENCY

In the evaluation framework *efficiency* is an idealised issue of static optimisation located within the analytical concerns of economic performance. The evaluative issues relate to the ways in which IB operations approach productive and allocative efficiency and, through this, the ultimate objectives of maximised welfare outcomes. The essential (even existential) issue here is that at any given point in time the world has a fixed quantity of potentially productive resources, so that the objective should be to secure the ability of these resources to maximise the (consumer validated) benefits from them. To approach these issues, mainstream IB theorising distinguishes two types and sources of potentially productive resources, with the efficiency outcomes then mediated by the relationships between the use of these resources as determined in MNE decision processes. Firstly, we have those attributes and assets possessed by the *firms* that provide their ability to organise and operationalise value-adding activities, their ownership advantages (OAs). The short-term objective of the MNE is to maximise the immediate returns they get from this fixed stock of OAs, under whatever current competitive and institutional conditions they have to operate. Secondly, the capacities of particular locations to provide effective inputs into value-added processes; these being an important aspect of, but crucially for this efficiency analysis only one facet of, location advantage (LAs).

This caveat regarding LAs immediately points to central perspectives in the discussion of the efficiency issue. MNEs will choose to carry out productive activities in a particular location in reflection of some combination of its currently accessible advantages, but these need not be ones that are conducive to the types of resource-usage efficiencies targeted by this evaluative criteria. An important practical manifestation of this point would relate to an interpretation of the extensive growth of FDI and international penetration of MNEs in the first post-war decades. Here it would have been easy to suggest that such an extensive and successful positioning of IB operations in the newly re-emergent international economy must have been a manifestation of dominant and pervasive efficiency. The elements of IB theorising that soon emerged to explain this new phenomenon, at the firm level, provided us with the ability, at least retrospectively, to refute any such a naive viewpoint and to position efficiency as a much more contingent and context-specific issue.

Certainly this influential and increasingly visible early growth of MNEs must have reflected very satisfactory performance in terms of their own accepted objectives: profitability, growth and the penetration of new markets. What our subsequent comprehension of IB now makes analytically clear, however, is that the source of this success was very unlikely to be efficient resource usage, but rather the effective exercise of market power. This reflected the prevalence of the market-seeking (MS) strategic imperative, whose necessity and viability was conditioned by factors relating to both OA and LA and to MNEs' organisation as multi-domestic hierarchies in, essentially, a pre-globalisation international economy. The crucially influential LA was the prevalence of trade restraints; imperfections in international final-product markets that served to isolate important national economies. This meant that firms with products likely to be competitive in these markets needed to opt for second-best production there, usually against a logical preference for supply through trade from a plausibly more efficient location. But at this early stage in the appearance of many post-war global industries, firms with the capacity to make this step into international production were very few, with powerfully hegemonic OAs. This meant that once they had taken the 'tariff jumping' response to the negative LAs they were often dominant in the market entered. Market power derived from very strong OAs allowed them to secure healthy profitability, without needing to achieve, or even be concerned with, optimal productive efficiency.

Indeed, as discussed in detail in Chapter 4 this mode of MS strategic positioning at the subsidiary level can be seen to be vulnerable to three sources of *inefficiency*. Firstly, the small size of the individual national markets to which a subsidiary's supply was normally constrained was likely to preclude the full potentials of economies of scale in production. Secondly, the problem of inappropriate technology transfer, reflecting the dependence of these operations on the OAs generated by their parent company. What the subsidiary needs to produce will reflect the *demand* structure of the host market, but the inherited production techniques (OA) may not match the *supply* conditions there. Inefficiencies may emerge if the technologies (generated to reflect *home*-country factor proportions) require too much of scarce and expensive *host*-country factors or are insufficiently oriented to the use of more readily available ones. Thirdly, there is a danger of X-inefficiency in these subsidiaries, in the sense that they may not be fully motivated to make the most effective use possible of the very effective OAs they have access to. Parent company decision makers may not have (or attempt to secure) access to all the information needed to judge the subsidiary's efficiency. The ability to return satisfactory seeming profits – and report a reasonable market share – may be deemed acceptable, in the absence of knowledge of such possible higher levels of efficiency and performance that are being foregone due to, for example, poor management, engineering or marketing.

Central to our analysis of how IB evolved through the latter decades of the twentieth century was the considerable diminution of these market imperfections that had allowed the MS MNEs to be profitable without needing to fully target efficiency. Firstly, the systemic lowering of tariff barriers and other trade restraints, in both developed industrial economies and those developing economies now seeking a genuinely competitive basis for industrialisation. Secondly, the rise of increasing numbers of new MNEs, sometimes from economies with long-standing roots in IB but increasingly from new source countries. This quickly undermined the hegemonic status of the OAs of the small group of post-war MNEs, and meant they found the need to pursue new ways of manifesting their competitiveness. Overall, the global markets in which all MNEs now operated had become much more competitively intense. The crucial short-run implications of this for the firms was that they did now need to address the most effective possible use of their current sources of competitiveness, their OAs. This benefitted efficiency in two ways; each element of their OAs needed to be operated in the ideal location and to fully achieve its productive potentials there. The now efficiency-seeking (ES) MNE needed to build up a global supply network producing each part of its product range in the optimal location and then securing fully efficient operations in each one. *Efficiency* now became the core priority of the short-run objectives of the MNE, getting best performance from its current competitive competences.

From the firm-level perspective, therefore, these developments in the global economy will have generated a move to ES strategies which should have secured the greater levels of operative efficiency required. This would, in fact, result from the ability to overcome each of the three inefficiencies innate to the MS environment. Since the ES subsidiaries are now parts of *global* supply *networks* they will have access to extensive international markets and should have no constraints in realising economies of scale. The need (and, presumably, increasingly the ability) to carry out each value-adding activity in the location whose most competitive input capacities match those required by the related technology should remove the danger of inefficiency due to inappropriate technology transfer. Lastly, each subsidiary now needs to continually validate its position in a supply network that is always open to reformulation and the reallocation of responsibilities. There is no longer scope to hide X-inefficiency.

From the point of view of national host economies we can see that those changes in their policies that serve to attract and facilitate MNEs' ES operations also address the objective of securing new levels of efficiency in their resource usage. Even for already industrialised and internationally oriented developed economies the participation in a more open global marketplace is likely to involve an acceptance of an increased role for ES operations. But the more dramatic and dynamic context is that of those economies addressing the possibilities of internationally competitive industrialisation for the first time – in effect those modelled in Kojima's scenario for trade-creating FDI. Here potentially productive resources, that had previously been unemployed or seriously underemployed (operating at levels of productivity well below their potential), are drawn into new supply operations that make full use of their innate capacities and target optimised efficiency. In theoretical terms the refocused MNE strategies are no longer attracted by negative LAs (reacting to market imperfections) but instead based on the activation of positive LAs (cost-competitive and efficient inputs). Overall, the ES strategies can be seen as part of the ways in which host economies are allowed to realise the full implementation of their sources of static comparative advantage.

Thus, in summary of the efficiency issues, it has been indicated (Pearce, 2006, 48) that if an MNE's 'operation in a particular location had found [there] *the* most productive LAs available to it worldwide (i.e., those that secure the most cost-effective use of [its] relevant OAs)' whilst, at the same time the MNE 'was making available a better package of OAs (i.e. capabilities to get the greatest value from the country's input potentials)' than could have been accessed from any other source, then this should be an optimising complementarity that, through efficiency maximisation, has the potential to raise 'world economic welfare to a level that could not have been achieved in any other way' (Pearce, 2006, 44). But this then points to our next evaluation issue. Where two independent agents provide inputs into a distinctive output how, and how fairly, will the rewards be distributed between them?

DISTRIBUTION

From that background it is, therefore, easy to conceptualise the basic nature of the *distribution* issue. Further meditation on its theoretical background soon suggests, however, the near impossibility of providing a convincing practical evaluative outcome in any particular real-world case. Crucially, the aim of distribution is not merely to achieve some sort of quantitative measure of how the rewards from a project are shared between the relevant parties, but to project an assessment of the 'fairness' or 'justice' of that outcome. Indeed, it may be fair to comment that the issue itself, as articulated here, has tended to provide more academic, theoretical and analytical interest than extensive practical concern in terms of the acceptance of MNEs' operations in many contexts.[1]

There may, in fact, be two reasons for the relatively limited actually observed dissent over the distribution outcomes relating to successful ES projects. Firstly, the expected distribution of benefits from such, mainly export-oriented, projects may have been defined and agreed between relevant parties prior to the setting up of the operation. Secondly, the level of success of the project may have ensured that both MNEs and host countries are satisfied with the outcome; ultimately, the distribution outcome reflects a 'satisficing' decision. Furthermore, this acceptance may also reflect the fact that neither party has fully informed knowledge of what rewards they might feel entitled to in a properly 'just' distribution. In ways to be discussed later it is a 'bounded rationality' acceptance. Meanwhile, it is useful to widen the context beyond the (most immediately indicative) one of ES operations to accept wider and more diverse objective functions by both MNEs and host economies.

We have seen in earlier chapters how the MNE's expectations from the operations of individual subsidiaries will differ according to their location and also evolve through time; involving some mix of contributions to ongoing current profitability and the longer-term development of the firm's global competitive positioning. Similarly, host-countries' expectations from MNE involvement,

> may include improved supply to local customers (quality and price of goods and services), improved conditions for local inputs (degree of usage and levels of rewards), improved achievement of short-run government policies (e.g. taxation, industrialisation, trade balance) and the provision of significant impetus to longer-run objectives in terms of sustainable growth and development. (Pearce, 2006, 50)

The objectives of both parties are clearly positioned within very different and ever-changing contexts, which may have allowed both of them to find sources of satisfaction in the shared outcome and to accept the continuation of the project, including its scope for change and repositioning. What this perspective does not allow is any form of meaningful shared and agreed 'measure of the overall level of achievement of the operation or, therefore, of any possible way of specifying what was the *actual* division of the outcome between [MNE] and host-country interests' (Pearce, 2006, 50–1).

It was then central to the more theoretically based concerns over distribution that, just as it was more-or-less impossible to provide a meaningful simple measure of an *actual* outcome, it was even further beyond logical feasibility to derive a comparable measure of what would have been a *fair* or *just* distribution. The implausible analytical desire would have been to compare an available indicator of the *actual* distribution with some hypothetical calculation of what would have been a *fair* outcome. The implicit driver of the early, and still persisting, concern with distribution was the suspicion that were such a comparison available it would indicate a gap between the two measures, and one that would be much more likely to favour the MNE. Beyond the scope of analytical rigour it is these types of perspective that have generated the more trenchant allegations that MNEs have often been able to 'exploit' host countries and, indeed, that the revised options opened up by the forces of globalisation have often enhanced these possibilities.

In the fraught philosophical territory of any attempt to conceptualise what might be considered a 'fair' distribution outcome in the case of, let us say, a successful (that is, efficient) ES production operation[2] it might be that determining an accurate market price for each value-adding input (OAs and LAs) would be the most realistic indicator. But both theory and observed practice would tell us that many of the most influential of such prices either cannot exist in any plausible market-determined form or might be subject to distortions; perhaps, very precisely, distortions that systematically negate any intuitive sense of fairness and even feed into just the sense of MNE 'exploitation' that has fuelled critiques. The latter possibility may derive from the fact that many operations, very notably the ES ones we focus on here, are established on the bases of bargaining processes with relevant host-economy decision makers and agencies. The potential for distributional distortions (reflected in implicit prices) here is likely to 'reflect a case of asymmetrical information [since MNEs] may be able to project superior knowledge of key factors in a bargaining process' (Pearce, 2006, 51).

In terms of the technological OAs defining an MNE's ability to operate an efficient production process the internalisation element of the theory makes clear that the firm will wish to retain exclusive access to this knowledge. Though it will proclaim the unique and distinctive potentials embodied in these OAs it will not, for 'seller uncertainty' reasons, be prepared to reveal any details of what these attributes are to host-country decision makers. The familiar arguments relating to market imperfections for intangible assets thus mean that no explicit prices will be invoked for these technological OAs. But, critics argue, the overall terms of MNE participation may nevertheless embody, in effect, rewards to the MNE that imply an excessive and 'unfair' price for these OAs. Another – less emphasised but quite indicative – advantage that MNEs may project to potential host countries in an ES bargaining process is the extent of their current international market and its growth potential. This would be a major attractive feature to a host country targeting export-oriented industrialisation. But again the host negotiators will be unlikely to have access to the information to validate the MNE's claims, either regarding its own global markets or those of rivals that may also be interested in the project. The host country may need to make a 'bounded rationality' evaluation of the MNE's claims and risk offering what may, in fact, be excessively generous terms. The ultimate danger here is then that MNEs may be 'overpaid' for their OAs through, for example, favourable tax arrangements and other forms of direct financial subsidisation.

Though the prices actually paid by ES MNEs for their local inputs are likely to be relatively open and transparent there often remains the suspicion that their determination may have been distorted in ways that compromise the fairness of the reward from their contribution to achieved operative efficiency. At one level these possibilities may be 'MNE-neutral' in that they merely manifest elements of government strategy and policies that are aiming to support a move towards effective export-oriented industrialisation by enhancing the competitiveness of natural sources of comparative advantage. MNEs may take advantage of these conditions simply because they possess the best OAs to do so. Once again, however, there is the potential for the firms to secure particular beneficial terms within bargaining processes, including not only preferred prices for labour, energy, raw materials and other local inputs but also regulatory supports such as repressive employment regulations.

In a somewhat ironic variant of asymmetrical information MNEs may attempt to claim better knowledge of the *relative* value of a host-country's LAs during an ES-based bargaining process. Unless the country is able to assert some very distinctive qualitative attributes in its input potentials an MNE may try to claim a more carefully informed *comparative* knowledge of rival economies (especially relating to the needs of its own technologies). From this it could suggest the (essentially 'footloose') potential for the location, or relocation, of its production operations elsewhere unless its particular terms are met. This, in fact, manifests a particular bargaining strength available to many MNEs once they are attuned to operating a carefully networked strategy in the globalised economy. In such ES operations, in particular, the MNEs can project both their own organisational flexibility and the capacity to base this on 'possession of better information on comparative productivity than would be available to an individual host-country government' (Pearce, 2006, 52). In fact, it is these potentials for MNEs to exercise well-informed flexibility in networks of globalised operations that provide the background to our next evaluative issue: their perceived ability to undermine the economic and political *sovereignty* of individual nation states.

SOVEREIGNTY

The process of globalisation has opened up extensive markets for capital, technology, skilled labour, intermediate goods and final products, so that national governments find themselves in international competition in terms of policies related to them. But then MNEs can be alleged to undermine the sovereignty of governments to implement policies in these areas, precisely because they are themselves major players in these international markets and often organise transactions within them through their own internalised networks. We can discern two dimensions to these concerns (Pearce, 2006, 55–6). Firstly, MNEs may be able to impose constraints on the ability of governments to secure the intended results from implemented policies in areas such as monetary and fiscal. Secondly, they may be able to lobby in ways that limit the flexibility of governments to even formulate meaningfully distinctive national policies in areas such as welfare and social provision or environmental regulations.

The most familiar, pervasive and publicly contentious of the first of these possibilities is, of course, the scope available to MNEs that are operating through integrated multi-country supply networks to exercise transfer pricing. Where an intermediate[3] good is transferred between two parts of the same company in different countries the reported price of the transaction can be at its own discretion. This enables it to determine, through the transfer price, where the operation's inherent profitability is actually reported for taxation purposes. If a country sought to raise extra revenue by increasing its profit-tax rate the MNE could simply reduce profits reported there by adjusting the relevant transfer prices. The ability of the country to achieve the objective of a sovereign policy is immediately negated.

An example of the potential for MNEs to undermine a country's sovereign policy discretion can also carry resonances with our previous discussion of the distribution issue. Whilst one objective of a government may be to attract new MNE investments so as to generate improved job opportunities, any related attempt to also determine favourable employment conditions supported by strong welfare policies may flounder. Thus 'minimum wage legislation, setting of particular standards for worker's

welfare, permission of active unionisation, and general attempts to determine employment conditions above levels' that MNEs suggest exceed
those prevailing elsewhere might be projected as reasons for not investing
(Pearce, 2006, 57). To secure one sovereign policy objective (higher levels
of employment) the government needs to abandon another (its view of
acceptable employment conditions).[4]

GROWTH AND DEVELOPMENT

The first element of this evaluation framework addressed the issue of MNEs'
effect on the *efficiency* of the use of the world's *fixed* stock of productive
resources at a point in time. But these resources will have, in different ways
and to varying degrees, dynamic potentials. Thus they can also be seen as possible sources of positive change and efficiency improvement through time.
Therefore, to complete the framework, we need to address this more dynamic
issue of how MNEs' operations relate to potential sources of change in the
global stock of productive capacities and capabilities over time; the analytical
concern is with *growth and development*. As we will see, an important aspect
of this issue, from the MNE perspective, will be how they are able to use their
diverse and always evolving operations in different locations as learning processes from which they can upgrade their competitive scopes; securing new
OAs to underpin their own growth and development.

But, as with the discussion of efficiency, the initial analytical focus can
usefully devolve into that of MNEs' operations in particular host economies and the nature of its involvement with their sources of competitiveness (their LAs). Will this participation be likely to support and help realise
that economy's potential for growth and development or be alienated by
any such changes? Here the key theoretical point is that a country's development implies, and depends upon, changes in its LAs. So the core of
the growth and development issue becomes how the MNEs will respond
to such changes in a country's LAs; will they reject them and alter their
commitments in negative ways or will they perceive and respond positively
to the newly redefined scopes? The efficiency issue implied that MNEs
operated in a particular location in the way that they did (efficiently or
inefficiently) because this seemed to be their most competitively relevant
response to the country's LAs at that precise moment in time. This part of
the growth and development issue thus asks how MNEs will respond when
the LAs that had defined their current operations change.

To begin the process of elaborating the varied possibilities of MNEs'
involvement in a host-country's growth and development we need to recognise that this will depend on what the current competitive bases of the

economy are and on the forms taken by the MNEs' participation in it. To distinguish and evaluate the possibilities that can then emerge we apply two typologies adopted in earlier chapters. Firstly, the categorisation of levels of resources (Pearce and Zhang, 2010; Zhang and Pearce, 2012; see Chapter 7 here) that reflect different states and stages in a country's development. Secondly, the typology of subsidiary roles and motivations that we have found (Chapter 7) to reflect the competitive diversity in MNEs' response to its heterogeneous and ever-changing competitive environment. We can then discern two broad dimensions to the possibilities. Can MNEs assist a country's growth and development by enabling it to get more extensive (quantitative) benefits from its current resource potentials? Or can MNEs support the generation of new potentials by providing (qualitative) opportunities for the upgrading of current resources (their more intensive use) or even the creation of significantly new ones?

In the resource-level typology, level-1 are natural and primary resources in the form of minerals, extracted energy or forestry, which immediately endow a country possessing them with an exploitable source of international competitiveness with the potential to drive the early phases of growth and development. As LAs these can then serve to attract the resource-seeking (RS)[5] motivation in MNEs. Historically, RS is often distinguished as the central motivation in the pioneering wave of FDI in the decades prior to World War I. This reflected the increasing need for such resources as inputs to the already fast-growing industrial economies. In the same way, we saw in the previous chapter how RS has become (an often government-mandated) priority in emerging Chinese FDI. Interestingly, both these cases reflect situations where RS FDI, in effect, mediates between the developmental needs or potentials of *both* the MNE's home country and that of the targeted resource-rich host. More generally IB theorising has distinguished the relevance of these types of level-1 resources as potential starting points for the sequence of integrated stages (for example, processing, refining, semi-manufacturing) that are internalised by a vertically integrated MNE.

As a *natural* endowment level-1 resources may well be the first exploitable potential available to a country seeking to commence an economic development that needs to be asserted around international competitiveness. Our analysis then suggests this potential for national growth and development needs to accept two constraints. Firstly, if the resource-based opportunities are indeed intended to be the first significant step in development the presumption would then be that the country lacks the relevant knowledge and expertise (in mining or plantation agriculture, for example) to initiate them and, at the same time, inadequate access to necessary amounts of capital. The extensive presence of MNEs in activating these projects then precisely reflects their possession of these facilitating competences; technology and experience, access to capital and, vitally, experience in the international markets for the primary resources. But this would then impose an intimidating degree of dependency on the country's development, with potentially negative implications regarding both distribution and sovereignty issues.

The second constraint is that we define level-1 resources as being either totally non-renewable or capable of being renewed only over long and uncertain periods of time. As a basis for growth and development they are inevitably unsustainable. Governments need to see beyond however effective *early* growth is, when based around these resources, to more sustainable sources and styles of development. One advocation in this regard was that such countries could gain more value from their level-1 resources by seeking the localisation of sequential stages in the value-chain building from them. Vertically integrated MNEs, with expertise in these subsequent stages, might be logical candidates to achieve this. But these firms might then be the first to point out to the host government that this localisation could be inefficient if these subsequent stages required inputs (for example, energy, labour skills) that the country did not possess. Also this forward integration would not delay the redundancy of the level-1 resources. Indeed, it could even speed it up and it would also mean that the amount of local value-added activity that became obsolescent would eventually be even more extensive. Usually more logical, therefore, was the alternative possibility of using strengths generated during a resource-exploitation stage (tax revenue, foreign exchange, international contacts and associations) to build the bases for diversification into other more sustainable sectors; most notably cost-competitive manufacturing based around what we distinguish as level-2 resources.

Such level-2 resources are inputs into established and mature production operations that can be upgraded within the ongoing process of development itself and thereby be an embedded element in its sustainability. Thus the labour force is a defining level-2 resource, since its incumbents can be retrained to higher skills, whilst new entrants should be more productive if they reflect continuing improvements in education standards. Energy supplies to industry are also a level-2 resource that should be constantly open to improvement in terms of both reliability and price.[6] In the same way the capacity of important aspects of infrastructure (transport systems, ports and airports, communications and IT networks) should be improved within development to reinforce the scopes of industrial competitiveness. Both the MS and ES strategic motivations of MNEs will require level-2 inputs. But the implications of how they do so are likely to be very different in terms of the 'growth and development' issue.

The fact that it is difficult to discern any decisively positive or negative growth or development implications for MS operations by MNEs reflects the inherent nature of this context as discussed in detail in Chapter 4. Though in some cases the intention of the high-protection import-substitution strategy in LDCs was to achieve infant-industry growth this was rarely secured on a sustainable basis and the strategy was soon abandoned with its inefficiency undermining any truly developmental potentials. Similarly, protectionist strategies in already industrialised economies (from the 1930s, for example) aimed to protect existing levels of employment and activity, with no logical expectation that this provided a basis for meaningful and sustainable growth. Where MNEs were 'complicit' in such strategies it was with the defensive motivation of sustaining profitability in a particular market. If that market *did* grow significantly through time it would also be a source of growth for the MNE. But not one derived from roots in its own strategic development, in terms of finding new sources of genuine competitiveness supportive of its more broadly based targets. In theoretical terms MS operations are driven by the need to respond to the negative LAs of protectionist policies. Though implementing MS supply will need local level-2 resources it is not the perceived competitive potentials of these that attracts the MNE (as a positive LA). Though the strength of the MNE's OAs may, in practice, bring about some productivity gains in local labour, for example, this is likely to be quite marginal and not of significance for growth and development for either the MNE or the host economy.

By contrast, precisely because improved *efficiency* is always likely to be a source of much more broadly based improvements in economic performance, analysis has placed the ES motivations at the core of a significant source of growth and development. Once again the model of 'trade-creating' FDI provides a useful analytical starting point for this allowing us to distinguish two phases of economic progress at the national level that respond to this MNE-driven motivation. Here the historical cases underpinning this model can distinguish a very fast phase of relatively 'easy' growth, during which the ES operations of MNEs draw previously unemployed (or seriously underemployed) labour and other level-2 resources into internationally competitive production. But, as discussed in Chapter 5, this phase can quickly reach its limits when full-employment of the level-2 resources causes cost increases (for example, high wage rates, or higher energy prices). This changes the LAs that originally attracted the MNEs with the implication of possible 'footloose' migration of the MNEs' ES activity.

But we can then invoke a second plausible phase of orderly and sustained development, that can encompass informed responses by both the host government and MNEs. Through reinvestment in the level-2 resources we saw how host countries can ensure that higher productivity levels validate their higher rewards; notably as labour gains the ability to exercise higher levels of skills and to carry out higher-value-added production processes. At the same time, as the MNEs increase their commitments to an efficient global supply network, they become more carefully responsive to changing LAs of individual economies, but in ways that have the potential to be positively supportive of such changes that are innate to development. 'Footloose' behaviour may, indeed, be endemic to the internal dynamics of ES MNEs, but with wider potentials than when depicted as simply the abandonment of a particular host country. In an idealised interpretation, the perpetual pursuit of the ideal efficiency location for each part of its product range by these MNEs could embed them within the growth and development of many countries in a dynamic global supply network.

Apart from the very idealised view of decision-making accuracy by ES MNEs and of logical policy progression by host countries, there are more deep-rooted reservations about the longer-term viability of this source of ES-based growth and development. Central to these we find issues of dependency. In the short-term it is dependent on the ability of an MNE to make use of upgraded level-2 resources through the relocation of an appropriate part of its *current* product range. But in the longer term, and in technologically dynamic industries, sustainability would then depend on the ability of the MNE to have created *new* elements of its product range that could be applied to further resource upgrading. Then, beyond this, there would be the wider issue of how much a policy of *national* economic development can accept prolonged dependency on foreign sources of technology-based progress. This precisely points to the innate limitation of level-2 resources; though they can be upgraded to play higher-value-added roles they do not themselves possess the capacity to generate the new knowledge-based opportunities they need to work within. Thus sustainable and sovereign national development will depend on the increasing ability to include creative innovation-oriented level-3 resources.

The aim of such level-3 resources would be to generate locally the new sources of knowledge-based value-adding potentials that can provide increasingly competitive ways of utilising the upgraded level-2 resources or, where relevant, of getting continued and enhanced value from level-1 resources. Obviously the most effective level-3 resources will be those that are built around very distinctive creative capacities (in science, technology, market research, engineering) and possess the ability to turn these into highly competitive new goods and services. The defining feature of a country's sustainable development becomes its ability to generate increasingly effective uses for its more standardised productive inputs. But, central to our concerns here, this may decisively change the nature of the country's relationship with MNEs, but not terminate it. If the country does escape from excessive dependency on MNEs' current technological capacities, their very success in creating the uniquely distinctive new knowledge potentials that allow them to do so may themselves become targets for the MNEs' own forward-looking learning and creative agendas.

Here we recall the two complementary strategic imperatives that an MNE needs to continually address. So far we have seen that how the MNEs' need to approach securing the optimal performance from their current competitive abilities (OAs) leads them to co-opt level-1 and/or level-2 host-country resources and questioned the implications of this for those countries' capacity to realise their potentials for economic growth. Then the second overarching need for the MNEs is to renew and revitalise these OAs as the key source of their longer-term competitive evolution. As increasing numbers of countries pursued the generation of level-3 resources as the basis for their development, MNEs soon recognised that their own learning processes needed to systematically tap into the different scopes being created in a range of locations. The emergence of KS as an MNE motivation accepted diverse creative opportunities as a new LA that is integral to the development of host countries. This intermeshing of developmental ambitions then defined the evaluative issue regarding MNEs and level-3 resources. The country seeks to build up these creative resources to feed into its own growth and development performance. Does any co-option of these resources by MNEs' KS strategies enhance or compromise the ability of the country to benefit from these resources in terms of its own competitive progress?

Once again precise calculation becomes infeasible. This would require comparison of the degree of growth through time that occurs due to the activation of level-3 resources under two sets of circumstances. Firstly, when at least some of them are operated in collaboration with MNE participation and, secondly, when this does not occur and they are activated within entirely independent local innovation processes. We can also see that this, in effect, incorporates a dynamic variant of the distribution issue. If, for example, an exploratory project based around a country's level-3 creative resources, but initiated and formulated by an MNE, does generate new knowledge with innovative potentials, is such development as is eventually achieved fairly distributed between the interests of the host country and the MNE? The innate empirical impenetrability of these questions is compounded by the intangible nature of the output of these innovation-oriented, but essentially exploratory, processes, encompassing less than fully understood but multifaceted potentials to feed into *future* programmes of growth and development. Here the crucial dichotomy is

between the capacity of new creative knowledge generation to be a source
for development in the domestic economy (whether or not as part of the
MNE's other operations there) or, at the same time, to be transferred elsewhere by the MNE to feed into other parts of its global programmes for
competitive renewal.

Though beyond rigorous quantification this last issue does provide a
useful analytical way forward, by pointing to the value of characterising
the institutions of the host country, and of the MNE, that participate in
these exploratory creative agendas and influence the ways in which their
output may feed into different developmental potentials. Here it will be
institutions and policies of a national system of innovation (NSI) that will
have the potential to generate new knowledge and opportunities that are
supportive of the competitiveness of *that* economy. They will also have the
potential to achieve, in themselves, such levels of international distinctiveness that they may attract the potential participation of MNEs' own KS
agendas. Such an NSI will inevitably involve the interdependencies and
interactions between a wide range of facilities and agents that seek to cover
relevant stages in an innovation process,[7] from purely abstract investigation through to the completion and marketing of a new product. Since
these are separable steps in the process, each addressing particular agendas
based on particular skills and knowledge, the central issue here reflects the
potential for an MNE to co-opt the distinctive national competences of
any of these stages without necessarily having a commitment to preceding
or subsequent ones.[8]

To get some perceptions of the nature of this MNE participation, and
its implications for the performance of the NSI (as an agent of *domestic*
growth and development), we can apply an immensely simplified dichotomy. Firstly, pure precompetitive investigation that explores speculative
or abstract agendas, with no specified innovation outcome formulated or
targeted but in the hope that some quite radical new knowledge *will* emerge
that can then be moved towards opportunities that can break significant
new competitive ground. Secondly, the actual innovation process itself, in
which various new potentials (in technology, market perceptions, engineering) do come together to complete development of a new good or service
and undertake its competitive initiation.

As an exemplar of the issues raised at the precompetitive phase of an
NSI we can take basic scientific research.[9] Such research is carried out
simply to resolve scientific issues that are 'defined by scientists whose commitment is entirely to the enhancement of the body of knowledge' defined
by their areas of specialisation. This means that there is 'no predetermined
perception in the articulation or implementation of basic research projects
of any specific commercial application' that is in sight, so that the work is

not being set up as 'an attempt to resolve a question defined by a particular problem within a firm's current product development or engineering operations' (Papanastassiou and Pearce, 2009, 147). Nevertheless, both firms and countries are likely to understand the potentials of basic research as a source of the more radical developmental potentials that will be needed to sustain longer-term competitive progress. From the country's point of view it is logical to see basic research as a significant element of a balanced and sustainable NSI, even though its own immediate concerns may seem a long way from the introduction of path-breaking new innovations to the market.

From this it can be perceived that the most successful NSI are, ultimately, those that are able to offer the distinctive and idiosyncratic breakthrough goods to the market, and that it is then likely that a key source of such challenging originality can begin with really radical new technological possibilities defined in basic research. The possession and nurturing of a world-class basis in highly specialised, but potentially highly valued, precompetitive research expertise is vital to a country's developmental progress. But such niche technology leadership is likely to be equally valued and sought by MNEs. Thus, MNEs with highly ambitious 'global innovation strategies' (Papanastassiou and Pearce, 2009, 142–6) are likely to have basic research operations (their own labs; R&D alliances; collaborations with local institutions such as universities) in a number of separate locations. Whilst each can tap into the specialised world-leading agendas of its host NSI in one of the areas of science plausibly relevant to its innovation, similar arrangements established in other locations will also tap into comparable and hopefully complementary expertise there. Getting full value from this network then requires persistent exchanges of information between them, with the ultimate objective of perceiving (at the group level) new innovation possibilities building on the synthesis of different new pieces of scientific knowledge.

In terms of the ability of basic research output to feed through to economic progress we can now see two very different routes forward.[10] For a fully self-contained NSI a crucial capacity would be to generate 'horizontal' mechanisms in which new scientific potentials are effectively moved through domestic industry into innovations that ultimately enhance that country's international competitiveness. But for laboratories with extensive MNE participation crucial output is likely to be primarily transferred into, initially, the networks of similarly oriented laboratories and then, hopefully, on into more committed MNE innovation programmes.

The concern here is, therefore, that the output of scientifically successful basic research in projects with dominant MNE participation will have very constrained scope to progress naturally through the domestic NSI into innovation there. The first recipients with the scope to spot any synergistic potential it may possess will be other parts of the parent MNE group.[11] Nevertheless, there may then be very positive potentials when it is addressed in this wider context. The assimilation of such a specific piece of scientific knowledge into the more diverse creative programmes of an MNE may enhance the possibility that it can become part of an active innovation process. Similarly, when activated in juxtaposition with the MNE's range of creative facilities and their diverse insights, the basic research output may, in effect, acquire greater innovative potentials than it would have been perceived to possess if constrained to the limited scopes of a domestic NSI. But where the high-value-added activity of finalising a major innovation and initiating its first supply facilities is located is then a decision for the MNE's global strategists. It is very unlikely to be influenced by the sources of early stage knowledge inputs, however much they may have helped define the result. It would only be a highly serendipitous outcome if the NSI of the basic research also became the location for pioneering supply; in effect there would be no sequential influence linking the R&D to the competitive output.[12]

We should, however, acknowledge that there might be offsetting benefits to an NSI from MNE participation in basic research. Firstly, it is likely to bring the benefits of extra funding: setting up new facilities, refurbishing aging laboratories, improving the employment conditions of scientists. Secondly, it may add interesting new challenges and dimensions to these researchers' work if the necessity to report frequently to other sister laboratories in the group actually opens them to new perspectives and opportunities. Thirdly, it is important to see these pure-science basic results as possessing characteristics of a public good. When communicated to other facilities in the group they also remain part of the knowledge base of the initiating laboratory; they retain an important potential for the future work and progress of these laboratories and may, indeed, diffuse to some degree (perhaps through personnel transfers or new local alliances) into the wider host-country NSI.

By the time we reach the second of our focal 'stages' in an NSI, that of the completion of the innovation process in the form of product development itself, the emphases will have changed in two fundamental ways by comparison with the precompetitive focus on (mainly scientific) abstract and exploratory investigation. It is now the targeting of a specific and clearly envisaged 'commercial' prospect that motivates all the key participants. It will mainly involve various types of human capital in interpreting and projecting new elements of their own expertise, drawn from earlier less precisely motivated investigation, as parts of emerging and increasingly ambitious innovative agendas. Also, this emphasises, in line with views discussed in earlier chapters (for example, the work of Vernon and of

Bartlett and Ghoshal), that successful finalisation of a product development process is likely to need strong inputs from several functional areas (science; market research; engineering; ambitious risk-taking management) and the ability to secure their effective collaborative interactions. A successful NSI will need to have generated high levels of forward-looking innovation-oriented expertise in these several (level-3) competences. But such distinctive capacities, manifested in visibly innovative facilities, will be another facet of the diverse competences MNEs will be seeking as inputs into their own 'globalised' approaches to knowledge access and application.

The primary means through which MNEs have come to place key elements of their own globally focused approach to innovation within individual NSI have been variants of creative KS subsidiaries. We can now see the pioneering formulation of such operations, the product mandate as having been a rather ad hoc and intuitive breakout by an individual subsidiary that finds itself, somewhat unexpectedly, with a new local-derived innovation potential and persuades the parent to mandate it to pursue it. The subsequent evolution of the concept has moved the positioning of such operations into a much more consciously articulated status within MNEs' increasingly globalised approach to their innovation targets.[13] Whilst the assumption was that PMs would have discovered the key sources of originality from within their host economy, the latter perspectives expected the subsidiaries to be the chosen locations for the *completion* of an innovation, some of the inputs to which were provided from other elements in its global KS networks.

An example of the latter positioning would be the role of a *regional* product mandate (RPM) in the second phase of the global innovation strategy as posited by Papanastassiou and Pearce (2009, 142–6). Here the first phase would have allowed the MNE to derive the outlines of a new product concept (NPC), which 'fully defines the essential nature of the major new service through which the innovation will extend the competitive scope of the firm and industry' (Papanastassiou and Pearce, 2009, 145). The breakthrough inputs into the ability to formulate the NPC will have been accessed from varied sources in precompetitive investigation, both in science (basic work) and deeply investigative market research. But acknowledging the diversity of the global marketplace, and the need to maximise the returns from a major NPC whilst it retains the full scope of its breakthrough originality, would point to the need to offer it to differentiated markets in responsively different formats. Thus RPMs in different areas may be provided with the basic information already defined into the NPC, but with a mandate to create a variant to optimise competitiveness in its distinctive environment. Doing this will still retain decisive roles for local technologists (interpreting and communicating the science), market researchers (individualising the product in ways responsive to the target market) and engineers (designing the prototype technology to make best use of local input structures). All of these would work with strong subsidiary management aiming to achieve the types of inter-functional collaborations that were advocated in earlier concepts of the innovation process.

This type of scenario clearly indicates a potential for these aspects of MNEs' KS programmes to provide a host-country NSI with enhanced capacity to see its innovation-oriented (level-3) attributes leveraged as sources of growth and development. The inputs provided by the MNE may benefit (and benefit from) the local expertise and information so as to generate new sources of international competitiveness and, complementing this, the more or less guaranteed access to the MNE's established global or regional markets can ensure this result. But though these factors indicate the 'way in which the interjection of MNEs' global programmes for technological and competitive enrichment can strengthen individual NSIs' it also shows how their need to do this on 'a selective basis can alter the balance of an NSI (between stages) and its content (what is done in a particular stage)' (Papanastassiou and Pearce, 2009, 159–60). Thus, though there are plausible arguments as to how these operations of MNEs can individually add strong elements of impetus to a country's innovative capacities, there are also important warnings as to its limited viability as a developmental strategy.

Certainly this will involve a new and risky type of dependency. The prolongation of an innovative subsidiary's success within an NSI will depend, firstly, on the capacity of its parent MNE to generate, through its wider KS programmes, the key elements of major new innovation potentials, for which it will seek the best finalising location. The capacity of the focal subsidiary to attract these new product potentials will then depend on its continued ability to project to the parent the persisting and, hopefully, enhanced in-house capabilities to complete the intended innovations. The direction taken by such a subsidiary is likely to be much more contingent on the needs of the MNE and the priorities of its competitive evolution than on the supportive inputs of the local NSI. There is, therefore, a danger of relatively shallow local roots in such subsidiaries, amounting to a potential for a type of 'footloose' relocation of innovative responsibilities to alternative facilities in other countries that are projecting different, perhaps more path-breaking, signs of inventiveness.

Ultimately, the ideal would be for the country to build a healthy degree of MNE product development participation into a more consciously balanced NSI that retains, in particular, a continued commitment to the types of basic research that can help define truly original localised sources of innovation. Here the learning potentials available to local personnel in MNE product development subsidiaries may endow them with the types of experience and know-how in innovation processes and procedures that can help them in relating back to identify new developmental potentials in the domestic NSI. This experience could help to achieve an integrating balance in the NSI that can draw new unformulated local possibilities into fully realised innovations that could define this country's own knowledge-based dynamic competitiveness.

IN CONCLUSION

Our narrative of the development of multinationals over the past half-century has led us to characterise their dominant contemporary concern as that of building international networks for both implementation and innovation that seek to leverage the differences between locations towards their own global competitiveness. During their multi-domestic era the main strategic objective of MNEs had been to use selected elements of their established competitiveness to embed their operation in distinctive and responsive ways in the markets of individual host economies. Then two key factors in the subsequent organisational evolution have been the opening of international markets for both final products and intermediates and these firms' increasing ability to operate in those markets and to internalise the benefits. An implication of this is that whilst their earlier mode of behaviour led MNEs to embed selected elements of their competences towards supply of a host-country market their focus now has become to embed selected elements of a country's supply capacities into their own international networks. This places MNEs as central to the processes of globalisation.

Globalisation is, of course, an abstraction. Though its many analysts can point to its successes or failures as a system, the benefits or penalties resulting from these will devolve, in different ways and to differing degrees, onto its many participant players and agents. The view we have offered of the competitive positioning of the contemporary MNE clearly places it as the agent that is most likely to be determining the manifold outcomes of globalisation. Its emergence into such a (sometimes almost hegemonic) status derives, we have seen, from its ability to draw different aspects of separate locations towards integral global strategic objectives. In terms of assessing the ramifications of such MNE performance, beyond the achievement of their own firm-specific objectives, the logical focus turned on its implications for the different needs and intentions of its chosen locations; simplified for interpretation here as national economies.

The virtue most commonly attributed to globalisation, often with an associated credit offered to MNEs' operations, is that of allocative and productive *efficiency*. In both cases (globalisation as a system and the ES networks of MNEs) the assumption is that it allows a country's sources of immediate comparative advantages to be activated towards international competitiveness. But our analysis tells us that the cases are not a perfect match; the ES behaviour of MNEs is not simply a natural subset of globalisation's expectations as its theorists postulated. In its pure macro-level trade-theory-based form globalisation sees a country selling its price-competitive exports into arm's-length international markets. Once IB introduces the MNE as the agent creating and activating this export process the trade will be predominantly organised intra-group and beyond the purview of normal market transactions. Now, in ways described in earlier parts of this chapter, issues of *distributive* fairness and economic and political *sovereignty* come decisively into play.

In national economies there are many sources of *growth and development*, depending on what stage the process has reached. But we have accepted here that its most likely sources of logically sustainable development are the generation of distinctive creative attributes that can fuel internationally competitive innovation. For MNEs our theory has suggested that internationalisation did not become viable until they had achieved (domestically) powerful products that could allow such expansion. But observation also indicated that once such firms had become MNEs then they widened their learning environment to encompass the knowledge scopes of many countries. Again innovation became the main driver of their developmental sustainability, but now they did this by involving themselves selectively within the unique creative potentials of host countries. The countries and the MNEs share agendas for learning and innovation and the two become increasingly interactive and interdependent. The question we have elaborated, and which still remains open for informed investigation, is whether MNE participation in elements of a country's creative endeavours increases the likelihood of those driving national competitiveness (new locally completed innovations generating trade success) or constrains and distorts it.

NOTES

1. The assertion here is that there is very little practical evidence of *successful* ES-type operations collapsing (or generating significant friction with local agencies) simply due to dissent over the perceived fairness of observed reward distribution.
2. In the alternative case of MS operations the issue may be more related to the distribution of 'losses' or, at least, the determination of who pays the penalty for inefficiencies. The challenge of the calculation (Pearce, 2006, 53–4) would be to assess how the rewards to

MNEs and host countries differ under these trade-restrained MS conditions from what they might have expected from supply of the same market under ideal circumstances.

3. This could include a final product assembled in a cost-competitive location and then transferred to the same group's marketing operations in a high-income country for sale.

4. At an extreme it could even be suggested (Pearce, 2006, 57) that MNEs might 'even project suspicion of the competitive implications of social democratic publicly financed welfare and social programmes as indicative of a climate unsympathetic to business interests.'

5. Our definition of RS focuses on *primary* resources only. It, therefore, differs from that of Dunning and Lundan (2008, 68) by excluding their 'cheap and well-motivated unskilled or semi-skilled labour', which becomes a key element of our level-2 resources.

6. Here the reference is to ability of the energy-supply system to provide energy to consumers and to industry, rather than the primary source of energy as a level-1 resource.

7. Manea and Pearce (2004, 111–12) suggest that a fully effective NSI would need to cover the full range of creative scopes from the basic research that can feed into the generation of new knowledge and derivation of 'new technical and commercial possibilities, to the ability to carry out effectively its commercial implementation through firms that have the complementary assets (entrepreneurial, financial, marketing and creative engineering) to bring this new knowledge successfully into economic practice'.

8. The MNE is likely to be involved with these stages but find reason to implement them elsewhere in a 'global innovation strategy' (Papanastassiou and Pearce, 2009).

9. This is not intended to endorse science as the only starting point for successful innovation. The potentials for market-driven innovation also lead MNEs to carry out exploratory market research in a range of different markets that have the potential to generate quite challenging perspectives on the future competitive directions of an industry. Nevertheless, pure scientific research may have the greater likelihood of fuelling radical innovations simply because it is carried out beyond any conditioning by the firms' current market commitments, to a degree unlikely to be fully matched by market research.

10. For the scientists themselves there is likely to be a very important alternative constituency for their output, in terms of communication with a wider peer group through academic publications and conferences.

11. Thus we can see that an MNE with 'a strong innovative culture is one with well-developed and mutually-creative inter-functional communications, in which research scientists can achieve valuable and uncompromised originality', but with the mechanisms for this to feed through to effective commercial breakthroughs (Papanastassiou and Pearce, 2009).

12. Such basic research laboratories may also be commissioned to carry out 'applied' research which 'continues to be based around the investigation of specific *scientific* questions' but with these now 'defined in the light of potential practical applications . . . that have been discerned within the results of basic research' (Papanastassiou and Pearce, 2009, 148). In terms of our dichotomy of innovation phases this is a hybrid role. The work is still done by research scientists but their agenda is now set by the perceived needs of other participants in the process with growing perceptions of competitive potentials.

13. Important examples include the 'strategic leader' of Bartlett and Ghoshal (1986) and the 'competence creating subsidiary' of Cantwell and Mudambi (2005).

Bibliography

Bain, J.S. (1956), *Barriers to New Competition*, Cambridge, MA: Harvard University Press.

Bartlett, C.A. and S. Ghoshal (1986), 'Tap your subsidiaries for global reach', *Harvard Business Review,* 64(6), 87–94.

Bartlett, C.A. and S. Ghoshal (1989), *Managing Across Borders: The Transnational Solution*, Boston, MA: Harvard Business School Press.

Bartlett, C.A. and S. Ghoshal (1990), 'Managing innovations in the transnational corporation', in C.A. Bartlett, Y.L. Doz and G. Hedlund (eds), *Managing the Global Firm*, London: Routledge.

Behrman, J.N. and W.A. Fischer (1980a), *Overseas R&D Activities of Transnational Companies,* Cambridge, MA: Oelgeschlager, Gunn & Hain.

Behrman, J.N. and W.A. Fischer (1980b), 'Transnational corporations: market orientations and R&D abroad', *Colombia Journal of World Business,* XV, 55–60.

Birkinshaw, J.M. (1994), 'Approaching heterarchy – a review of the literature on multinational strategy and structure', *Advances in International Comparative Management*, 9, 111–44.

Birkinshaw, J.M. and A.J. Morrison (1995), 'Configurations of strategy and structure in subsidiaries of multinational corporations', *Journal of International Business Studies*, 26(4), 729–54.

Buckley, P.J. (1990), 'Problems and developments in the core theory of international business', *Journal of International Business Studies*, 21, 657–66.

Buckley, P.J. (2004), 'The role of China in the global strategy of multinational enterprises', *Journal of Chinese Economic and Business Studies*, 2(1), 1–25.

Buckley, P.J. and M.C. Casson (1976), *The Future of the Multinational Enterprise*, London: Macmillan.

Buckley, P.J., J. Clegg, A. Cross, X. Liu, H. Voss and P. Zheng (2007), 'The determinants of Chinese outward foreign direct investment', *Journal of International Business Studies*, 38(4), 499–518.

Buckley, P.J., L.J. Clegg, A.R. Cross and H. Voss (2010), 'What can emerging markets learn from the outward investment policies of advanced countries?', in K.P. Sauvant, G. McAllister with W.A. Maschek (eds),

Foreign Direct Investments from Emerging Markets: The Challenges Ahead, New York: Palgrave Macmillan.

Buckley, P.J., H. Voss, A. Cross and L.J. Clegg (2011), 'The emergence of Chinese firms as multinationals: the influence of the home institutional environment', in R. Pearce (ed.), *China and the Multinationals: International Business and the Entry of China into the Global Economy*, Cheltenham: Edward Elgar.

Burenstam-Linder, S. (1961), *An Essay on Trade and Transformation*, London: Wiley.

Cantwell, J. (2000), 'A survey of theories of international production', in C.N. Pitelis and R. Sugden (eds), *The Nature of the Transnational Firm* (2nd ed.), London: Routledge.

Cantwell, J.A. and R. Mudambi (2005), 'MNE competence-creating subsidiary mandates', *Strategic Management Journal*, 26(12), 1109–28.

Coase, R.H. (1937), 'The nature of the firm', *Economica*, 1, 386–405.

Cross, A., P. Buckley, J. Clegg, H. Voss, M. Rhodes, P. Zheng and X. Lui (2007), 'An econometric investigation of Chinese outward direct investment', in J.H. Dunning and T.M. Lin (eds), *Multinational Enterprises and Emerging Challenges of the 21st Century,* Cheltenham: Edward Elgar.

D'Cruz, J. (1986), 'Strategic management of subsidiaries', in H. Etemad and L. Séguin Dulude (eds), *Managing the Multinational Subsidiary*, London: Croom Helm.

Dunning, J.H. (1958), *American Investment in British Manufacturing Industry*, London: Allen and Unwin.

Dunning, J.H. (ed.) (1971), *The Multinational Enterprise*, London: Allen and Unwin.

Dunning, J.H. (1977), 'Trade, location of economic activity and the multinational enterprise: a search for an eclectic approach', in B. Ohlin, P.O. Hesselborn and P.M. Wijkman (eds), *The International Allocation of Economic Activity*, London: Macmillan.

Dunning, J.H. (1988), *Explaining International Production*, London: Unwin Hyman.

Dunning, J.H. (1993), *Multinational Enterprises and the Global Economy,* Wokingham: Addison-Wesley.

Dunning, J.H. (2000), 'The eclectic paradigm as an envelope for economic and business theories of MNE activity', *International Business Review*, 9, 163–90.

Dunning, J.H. (2002), 'Relational assets, networks and international business activity', in F. Contractor and P. Lorange (eds), *Cooperative Strategies and Alliances*, Amsterdam and Oxford: Elsevier Science.

Dunning, J.H. and S.M. Lundan (2008), *Multinational Enterprises and the Global Economy* (2nd ed.), Cheltenham: Edward Elgar.

Dunning, J.H. and R. Pearce (1994), 'The nature and growth of TNCs', in C. Nobes and R. Parker (eds), *Comparative International Accounting*, (4th ed.), Oxford: Allen.

Dunning, J.H. and A.M. Rugman (1985), 'The influence of Hymer's dissertation on the theory of foreign direct investment', *American Economic Review*, 75(2), 228–32.

Eden, L. and D. Li (2010), 'Rethinking the O in Dunning's OLI/Eclectic Paradigm', *The Multinational Business Review*, 18(2), 13–34.

Flowers, E.B. (1976), 'Oligopolistic reaction in European and Canadian direct investment in the United States', *Journal of International Business Studies*, 1, 43–55.

Graham, E.M. (1978), 'Transatlantic investment by multinational firms: a rivalistic phenomenon?', *Journal of Post Keynesian Economics*, 1(1), 82–99.

Håkanson, L. (1981), 'Organisation and evolution of foreign R&D in Swedish multinationals', *Geografiska Annaler*, 63B, 47–56.

Haug, P., N. Hood and S. Young (1983), 'R&D intensity in the affiliates of US-owned electronics companies manufacturing in Scotland', *Regional Studies*, 17, 383–92.

Hedlund, G. (1986), 'The hypermodern MNC: a heterarchy?', *Human Resource Management*, 25, 9–35.

Hedlund, G. (1993), 'Assumptions of hierarchy and heterarchy, with applications to the management of the multinational corporation', in S. Ghoshal and E. Westney (eds), *Organisation Theory and the Multinational Corporation*, London: Macmillan.

Hedlund, G. and D. Rolander (1990), 'Action in heterarchies – new approaches to managing the MNC', in C.A. Bartlett, Y. Doz and G. Hedlund (eds), *Managing the Global Firm*, London: Routledge.

Hewitt, G. (1980), 'Research and development performed abroad by US manufacturing multinationals', *Kyklos*, 33, 308–26.

Hirschey, R.C. and R.E. Caves (1981), 'Internationalisation of research and transfer of technology by multinationals', *Oxford Bulletin of Economics and Statistics*, 42(2), 115–30.

Hirschman, A.O. (1969), *How to Divest in Latin America and Why*, *Essays in International Finance*, Princeton, NJ: Princeton University Press.

Hood, N. and S. Young (1982), 'US multinational R&D: corporate strategies and policy implications for the UK', *Multinational Business*, 2, 10–23.

Hufbauer, G.C. (1966), *Synthetic Materials and the Theory of International Trade*, London: Duckworth.

Hymer, S. (1960/1976), *The International Operations of National Firms: A Study of Direct Investment*, PhD Thesis, MIT, Published 1976, Harvard, Cambridge, MA: MIT Press.

Hymer, S. (1970), 'The efficiency (contradictions) of multinational corporations', *American Economic Review – Papers and Proceedings*, LX(2), 441–8.

Hymer, S. (1972), 'The multinational corporation and the law of uneven development', in J. Bhagwati (ed.), *Economics and World Order from the 1970s to the 1990s*, London: Macmillan.

Kindleberger, C.P. (1969), *American Business Abroad: Six Lectures in Direct Investment*, New Haven: Yale University Press.

Kindleberger, C.P. (ed.) (1970), *The International Corporation – A Symposium*, Cambridge, MA: The MIT Press.

Knickerbocker, F.T. (1973), *Oligopolistic Reaction and the Multinational Enterprise*, Cambridge, MA: Harvard University Press.

Kojima, K. (1973), 'Reorganisation of north-south trade: Japan's foreign economic policy for the 1970s', *Hitotsubashi Journal of Economics*, 13, 1–28.

Kojima, K. (1978), *Direct Foreign Investment: A Japanese Model of Multinational Business Operations*, London: Croom Helm.

Kojima, K. (1982), 'Macroeconomic versus international business approach to foreign direct investment', *Hitotsubashi Journal of Economics*, 23, 630–40.

Kumar, N. (1996), 'Intellectual property protection, market orientation and location of overseas R&D activities by multinational enterprises', *World Development*, 24, 673–88.

Lall, S. (1979), 'The international allocation of research activity by US multinationals', *Oxford Bulletin of Economics and Statistics*, 41, 313–31.

Lu, J., X. Liu, M. Wright and I. Filatotchev (2014), 'International experience and FDI location choices of Chinese firms: the moderating effects of home-country government support and host-country institutions', *Journal of International Business Studies*, 45, 428–49.

Lundan, S.M. (2010), 'What are ownership advantages?', *The Multinational Business Review*, 18(2), 51–69.

Luo, Y., Q. Xue and B. Han (2010), 'How emerging market governments promote outward FDI: experience from China', *Journal of World Business*, 45(1), 68–79.

Manea, J. and R. Pearce (2004), *Multinationals and Transition: Business Strategies, Technology and Transformation in Central and Eastern Europe*, Basingstoke: Palgrave Macmillan.

Mansfield, E.D., D. Teece and A. Romeo (1979), 'Overseas research and development by US-based firms', *Economica*, 46, 187–96.

Mathews, J.A. (2002), 'Competitive advantages of the latecomer firms: a resource-based account of industrial catch-up strategies', *Asia Pacific Journal of Management*, 19, 467–88.

Mathews, J.A. (2006a), 'Dragon multinationals: new players in 21st century globalisation', *Asia Pacific Journal of Management*, 23, 5–27.

Mathews, J.A. (2006b), 'Catch-up strategies and the latecomer effect in industrial development', *New Political Economy*, 11(3), 313–35.

Moyo, D. (2012), *Winner Takes All: China's Race for Resources and What It Means for the World*, New York: Basic Books.

Narula, R. (2006), 'Globalisation, new ecologies, new zoologies, and the purported death of the eclectic paradigm', *Asia Pacific Journal of Management*, 23, 143–51.

Narula, R. (2012), 'Do we need different frameworks to explain infant MNEs from developing countries?', *Global Strategy Journal*, 2, 188–204.

North, D.C. (1990), *Institutions, Institutional Change and Economic Performance*, Cambridge: Cambridge University Press.

Ozawa, T. (1979a), *Multinationalism, Japanese Style: The Political Economy of Outward Dependency*, Princeton, NJ: Princeton University Press.

Ozawa, T. (1979b), 'International investment and industrial structure: new theoretical implications from the Japanese experience', *Oxford Economic Papers*, 72–92.

Ozawa, T. (1991), 'Japan in a new phase of multinationalism and industrial upgrading: functional integration of trade, growth and foreign direct investment', *Journal of World Trade*, 25, 43–60.

Papanastassiou, M. and R. Pearce (1997), 'Firm-strategies and the research intensity of US MNEs' overseas operations: an analysis of host-country determinants', in R. Pearce (ed.), *Global Competition and Technology*, Basingstoke: Macmillan.

Papanastassiou, M. and R. Pearce (1998), 'Individualism and interdependence in the technological development of MNEs; the strategic positioning of R&D in overseas subsidiaries', in J. Birkinshaw and N. Hood (eds), *Multinational Corporate Evolution and Subsidiary Development*, London: Macmillan.

Papanastassiou, M. and R. Pearce (1999), *Multinationals, Technology and National Competitiveness*, Cheltenham: Edward Elgar.

Papanastassiou, M. and R. Pearce (2009), *The Strategic Development of Multinationals: Subsidiaries and Innovation*, London: Palgrave.

Pearce, R. (1989), *The Internationalisation of Research and Development by Multinational Enterprises*, Basingstoke: Macmillan.

Pearce, R. (1999), 'The evolution of technology in multinational enterprises: the role of creative subsidiaries', *International Business Review*, 8(2), 125–48.

Pearce, R. (2006), 'Globalisation and development: an international business strategy approach', *Transnational Corporations*, 15(1), 39–74.

Pearce, R. and M. Papanastassiou (1999), 'Overseas R&D and the strategic evolution of MNEs: evidence from laboratories in the UK', *Research Policy,* 28(1), 23–41.

Pearce, R. and M. Papanastassiou (2006), 'To "Almost see the World": hierarchy and strategy in Hymer's view of the multinational', *International Business Review*, 15(2), 151–65.

Pearce, R. and S. Zhang (2010), 'Multinationals' strategies for global competitiveness and the sustainability of development in national economies', *Asian Business and Management*, 9(4), 1–18.

Peng, M.W., S-H. Lee and P.Y.L. Wang (2005), 'What determines the scope of the firm over time? A focus on institutional relatedness', *Academy of Management Review*, 30(3), 622–33.

Posner, M.V. (1961), 'International Trade and technical change', *Oxford Economic Papers,* 13, 323–41.

Poynter, T.A. and A.M. Rugman (1982), 'World product mandates: how will multinationals respond?', *Business Quarterly,* 47(3), 54–61.

Ronstadt, R.C. (1977), *Research and Development Abroad by US Multinationals*, New York: Praeger.

Ronstadt, R.C. (1978), 'International R&D: the establishment and evolution of R&D abroad in seven US multinationals', *Journal of International Business Studies*, 9(1), 7–24.

Rugman, A.M. (1981), *Inside the Multinationals*, London: Croom Helm.

Rugman, A.M. (1983), 'Multinational enterprises and world product mandates', in A.M. Rugman (ed.), *Multinationals and Technology Transfer: The Canadian Experience*, New York: Praeger.

Rugman, A.M. (2010), 'Reconciling internalisation theory and the eclectic paradigm', *The Multinational Business Review*, 18(2), 1–12.

Rugman, A.M. and A. Verbeke (2009), 'Location, competitiveness and the multinational enterprise', in A.M. Rugman (ed.), *The Oxford Handbook of International Business* (2nd ed.), Oxford: Oxford University Press.

Rugman, A.M., A. Verbeke and Q.T.K. Nguyen (2011), 'Fifty years of international business theory and beyond', *Management International Review*, 51(6), 755–86.

Tang, Y. (2014), *The Operations of Chinese Infrastructure Multinationals in Africa: Mediating Two Development Processes*, PhD Thesis, University of Reading.

Tang, Y. and R. Pearce (2011), 'The political economy of infrastructure multinationals: the case of Chinese investment in Africa', in R. Pearce (ed.), *China and the Multinationals: International Business and the Entry of China into the Global Economy,* Cheltenham: Edward Elgar.

Tang, Y. and R. Pearce (2014), 'The "how" and "why" of Chinese infrastructure MNEs' operations in Africa – an analytical framework', paper presented at the Annual Conference of the UK Academy of International Business – University of York.

Tang, Y. and R. Pearce (2017), 'The growth of Chinese multinationals: a micro-macro, FSA-CSA framework', in K. Ibeh et al. (eds), *Growth Frontiers in International Business*, Basingstoke: Palgrave.

US Tariff Commission (1973), *Implications of Multinational Firms for World Trade and Investment and for US Trade and Labor*, Report of the US Senate, Committee on Finance, Subcommittee on International Trade, Washington: US Government Printing Office.

Vaupel, J.W. and J.P. Curhan (1969), *The Making of a Multinational Enterprise*, Cambridge, MA: Harvard University Press.

Vaupel, J.W. and J.P. Curhan (1974), *The World's Largest Multinational Enterprises*, Cambridge, MA: Harvard University Press.

Vernon, R. (1966), 'International investment and international trade in the product cycle', *Quarterly Journal of Economics*, 80(2), 190–207.

Vernon, R. (1979), 'The product cycle hypothesis in a new international environment', *Oxford Bulletin of Economics and Statistics*, 41(4), 255–67.

Voss, H. (2011), *The Determinants of Chinese Outward Direct Investment*, Cheltenham: Edward Elgar.

Wang, C., J. Hong, M. Kafouras and M. Wright (2012), 'Exploring the role of government in outward FDI from emerging economies', *Journal of International Business Studies*, 43(7), 655–76.

White, R.E. and T.A. Poynter (1984), 'Strategies for foreign-owned subsidiaries in Canada', *Business Quarterly*, 59–69.

Williamson, O.E. (1975), *Markets and Hierarchies: Analysis and Antitrust Implications*, New York: Free Press.

Williamson, O.E. (1979), 'Transaction cost economics: the governance of contractual relations', *Journal of Law and Economics*, 22, 236–61.

Williamson, O.E. (1985), *The Economic Institutions of Capitalism*, New York: Free Press.

Yamin, M. (2000), 'A critical re-evaluation of Hymer's contribution to the theory of the transnational corporation', in C.N. Pitelis and R. Sugden (eds), *The Nature of the Transnational Firm* (2nd ed.), London: Routledge.

Zejan, M.C. (1990), 'R&D activities in affiliates of Swedish multinational enterprises', *Scandinavian Journal of Economics*, 93, 487–500.

Zhang, S. and R. Pearce (2012), *Multinationals in China – Business Strategy, Technology and Economic Development*, Basingstoke: Palgrave Macmillan.

Index

Printed and bound by CPI Group (UK) Ltd, Croydon, CR0 4YY

23/04/2025

14660980-0005